A Step of

FAITH

The History of the
Durham Rescue Mission

Reaching Out to Those in Need
Since 1974

ANDREA HIGGINS

Published by Durham Rescue Mission
Cover Design and Layout by thankful voice publishing, Hillsborough, NC
Printed by Strawbridge Studios, Inc., Durham, NC

A Step of Faith: The History of the Durham Rescue Mission

Published by Durham Rescue Mission, PO Box 11858, Durham, NC 27703.

Cover Design and Layout by thankful voice publishing, a ministry of Welcome Baptist Church, 3100 New Sharon Church Rd., Hillsborough, NC 27278.

Printed by Strawbridge Studios, Inc., PO Box 3005, Durham, NC, 27715-3005.

Library of Congress Control Number: 2006908194

Printed in the United States of America

Dedication

This book is lovingly dedicated to Norman Pollard, who took the time to show a young man named Ernie Mills that Jesus Christ is the way to salvation, and also to the thousands of volunteers who have donated incalculable hours and innumerable talents to the Durham Rescue Mission. The support of so many in the community—public officials,

Norman Pollard

corporations, churches, civic and school groups, and individuals—has helped make possible the Durham Rescue Mission's 30+-year-history of service to God and mankind.

Table of Contents

s we look back over the 30 years since the beginning of the Durham Rescue Mission, we are extremely privileged to have the favor of God and the friendship of Brother Ernie and Sister Gail Mills, and their staff at the Durham Rescue Mission.

Through the wisdom of God, we are witnessing a type of metamorphosis, from caterpillar to butterfly; where we see lives moving from a state of desperately destitute to a point where they are delightful in their destiny.

From the staff who supports to a society who sustains, souls are saved. Lives are liberated and emancipated from the entanglements and entrapments that erode the value of self worth, and rob a man or woman or child of a sense of dignity. The Durham Rescue Mission, by God's grace, has made a difference. Your compassion and contributions have made up the difference.

We are grateful about what God has done here. In 2004—just to realize what has transpired here—58,969 nights of lodging were provided. Now you try to pay for that hotel bill. It is tremendous. And 183,111 meals were served. That didn't count the ones that were wrapped up and taken home. Many were. Over 200,000 articles of clothing were issued out. During our backpack to school event, over 2,300 kids came to the Rescue Mission for help, and they were given the supplies to go into a classroom and be able to learn the things that were set before them. Just last year, over $3,100,000 worth of goods and services has been returned to our community.

Four hundred and twenty people made professions of faith in Jesus Christ the Lord. What a great testimony. Folks are on their way to heaven.

Brother Mills has had some discernment. He has had a spirit of direction. He knew that what God had called for, surely He would provide.

As Bucky Waters, my good friend, and great friend to the Mission, put it, 'These folks have a spirit of endurance.' It is with grateful hearts that we look back on the first 30 years of their work here, and look ahead as we embark on a wonderful opportunity to triple the number of women and children the Mission serves. We are so thankful to the Lord for His mercy and for His overwhelming grace. He saves us. He allows us to come into His service as sons and daughters to demonstrate His love, as Ernie and Gail have done for more than 30 years here in Durham.

Aaron Gamble
Pastor, Lighthouse Baptist Church, Durham, NC
Durham Rescue Mission Board Member

Author's Note

From a place with the unlikely name of Frog Level to people that couldn't have more appropriate names—like "Keg" Mills, Mr. Venerable and Mrs. Humbles—this story is filled with unforgettable characters and events that illustrate the merciful guiding hand of an almighty God. There was old Mr. Tilly standing at the well, and agreeing to let the mission till his land for a garden; and the larger than life Rev. H. L. Mickle, whose very different contributions nonetheless helped further the Mission. Their images are as endearing as they are enduring.

In the course of writing this book, Ernie Mills decided that he would like to mention by name the gentleman who kindly took Ernie and Gail on as oil customers when they first moved to Durham to start a rescue mission. That man's name, appropriately enough, was Don Christian, and his actions were special because no oil companies were taking on new customers during OPEC's oppressive oil embargo which had squelched supplies world-wide.

The very next day, after Ernie added his name to the book, the Mission received an unexpected visit from Don Christian's son, Steve, who wanted to tell the couple how his family loves the Mission and watched its progress through the years. He also handed Ernie a $5,000 check.

While collecting information for the book, mostly through oral history, there were many times when I facetiously accused Ernie, "You made that up!" because of unbelievable "coincidences" just like that one. But, of course, it was all true, well-documented and further testimony that a coincidence is a small miracle where God chooses to remain anonymous. All things work together for good, Ernie would invariably say, quoting scripture as we worked through describing how obstacles fell away as they kept their minds on God's Word. Through the telling of this story and highlighting the many large and small miracles that permeate the creation and endurance of the Durham Rescue Mission, it is our hope that everyone will see what God has done and what He offers all of us through his grace alone.

I also want to thank Ernie and Gail Mills for trusting someone who, as a new Christian, felt entirely ill-equipped to tell their amazing story of faith. They assured me that God doesn't call the qualified. He qualifies the called. It has been a privilege to document lives lived with such faith and generosity. Many have learned from them that to give is truly to receive—and that prayer changes everything.

—Andrea Higgins

Acknowledgments

*T*hank you to Durham Rescue Mission Executive Secretary Lois Cooper for patiently working out times for Ernie and Gail Mills to meet with the author—an almost impossible undertaking given their demanding schedule. Thanks also to Assistant Development Director Donna Mickle for finding so many hard-to-track-down, and all-but-lost details, and to Bookkeeper Ruth Everett who was always ready with a precise number to fill in the blank. A special thank you also goes to Donna's mother-in-law, Virginia "Nannie" Mickle, wife of the late Rev. H. L. Mickle, for sharing her treasured memories and photographs of the couple's long friendship with the Mission. And, finally, thanks to all those who shared their compelling personal testimonies that demonstrate God's perfect plan for every life.

Introduction
HOME FOR THE HOMELESS, HOPE FOR THE HOPELESS

Durham Rescue Mission is 30 years old.

*W*hen saw we thee a stranger, and took thee in? or naked, and clothed thee? Or when saw we thee sick, or in prison, and came unto thee? And the King shall answer and say unto them, Verily I say unto you, Inasmuch as ye have done it unto one of the least of these my brethren, ye have done it unto me.

—Matthew 25:38–40

"Oh my God, what *am* I doing with my life?"

Lynn Holloway sat injured on the side of the road where he had been hit by a car, thinking nobody cared if he lived or died. He had no idea the

This is where lives are changed!

plaintive question—and of whom he asked it—would be singularly appropriate in defining the direction of his life.

That night in 1994, the 39-year-old crack cocaine addict tried to get up from the street, but quickly fell back down. He crawled through a puddle to get to the curb and out of traffic. Through the dizziness caused from hitting his head on the pavement, he felt a sharp pain in his shoulder. As disoriented as he was, another thing was painfully clear: he had surrendered his life to crack.

Things had deteriorated so much for the hapless drifter that he was even being evicted from the "crack hotel" where he was staying in Durham, North Carolina.

Once again, he had smoked up the paycheck he earned as an ironworker on a construction site. He was out of money and out on the streets. Feet resting in that puddle, incoherent images of the confused path that led him to this soggy, sorry mess swam across his memory as all hope ebbed away.

As a boy in the Blue Ridge Mountain city of Asheville, North Carolina, Holloway never knew his father, who left when he was very young. Holloway dropped out of high school because he liked the idea of having his own money and being able to afford clothes that weren't second-hand. His boss fired him when he found out he quit school, and his mother wouldn't let him live at home if he refused to go back to school or at least get another job. He did neither, and that was the first time he was homeless. At 19, he got his GED and began a two-year stint in the Navy, where drugs were plentifully available if he wanted them.

Stationed in California while in the Navy, he stayed on there after he left the military. A family member introduced him to crack. Predictably, it turned into a love-hate relationship that would ultimately destroy his marriage, his career, and any feelings of self worth.

"It's devastating. It starts out like it's pleasurable. You get the idea you can handle it because it's such a high. Slowly it goes downhill. It makes you paranoid. You begin to spend more and more money and more and more time chasing it than tending to your responsibilities," Holloway said. "Eventually you start having two sets of friends. You're living two lives. You don't want your work friends to know you're doing it. The money is not there because you've spent it all up."

Tired of his habit, his wife kicked him out of the house where they lived in Portland, Oregon. In search of his precious high, he was even willing to leave little two-year-old Rebecca, his daughter, whom he adored. He landed back in Los Angeles where, as he describes it, he had his "ultimate run-in with drugs."

His drug use went from exciting entertainment to a desperate daily necessity. He lived the familiar downward spiral of addiction. Every time he landed work with his ironworking skills, he was bounced right off the job because of his reputation as a crack addict. He realized his life was headed off course, but it didn't stop him from seeking his next fix.

He lived in his truck until the police impounded it, and then he was on the streets. In between various attempts at recovery, he'd collect unemployment checks and eventually find a dealer. His brother came out to Los Angeles to work for a while, and when he headed back home to North Carolina, Holloway joined him.

Back in Asheville, Holloway looked for work and tried to stop using drugs. He cleaned up his act for a while and got a job re-facing the library at Duke University in Durham. That's when he fell back into drugs.

With no money and nowhere in particular to go, he had decided to go for a walk. While crossing busy Hillsborough Street, a major thoroughfare in Durham, Holloway was hit by that car, which sped off. He learned later that the driver did call for help, but at the time, Holloway thought he'd been left for dead.

"I'm ready to die. I was having my own pity party. I'm fed up with this life, the way I've been living," he recalled.

In shock and immobilized, Holloway watched the next series of events through a surreal haze. He remembers a police officer putting her comforting hand on his shoulder but not saying a word. Her tenderness gave him a sense of peace that everything was going to be alright. Then, harsh reality set in. Emergency medical technicians strapped him none too gently and far too tightly onto the gurney. When he complained of their rough treatment, they snapped at him to "shut up."

"I began to cry in that ambulance—and I guess I hadn't cried in years," Holloway said. "I remembered my mother's Bible studies, and I called on God. I didn't know I was making a vow, but I made a vow to God that, 'Lord, if you take this addiction from me, I will serve you for the rest of my life.' I really wanted the Lord to take me out of this addiction."

At Duke University Hospital Emergency Room, his dislocated shoulder was put in a sling. He was sent on his way once doctors were assured he did not have a concussion. At dawn, he went to the hotel where he had been staying to pick up his meager collection of clothing. Next, he headed to his VA counselor. With nowhere else to send him, she gave him bus fare and told him to go to the Durham Rescue Mission.

Within a couple of days, Mission Chaplain, the Rev. Barry Crowley shared the Gospel with Holloway. He finally understood God's plan of salvation, and how it related to him.

He became a Christian, and this time he willingly surrendered his life—but it was to God, not to the insatiable demon of addiction that robbed him of everything.

With the help of a scholarship from the Durham Rescue Mission, Holloway attended and graduated from Piedmont Baptist College in Winston-Salem, North Carolina and became a Christian counselor at the Durham Rescue Mission. He went on to become director of education, overseeing the Victory Program (the addiction recovery program for men).

He repaired his relationship with his ex-wife, becoming best friends, and he is once again part of his daughter's life.

* * * * * * * *

In 2004, the Rev. Ernie Mills and his wife, Gail, celebrated 30 years of helping people like Holloway get back on their feet. Together, the couple co-founded the Durham Rescue Mission in November of 1974 with a goal of offering homeless people hope, not just a hot meal and a warm place to sleep for a night.

Lynn and daughter, Rebecca, visiting Duke's Cameron Indoor Stadium. Lynn praises the Lord that he is renewing his relationship with Rebecca.

Before 1974, a person down on his luck in Durham simply found his way under the nearest bridge to get out of the rain or scorching sun. Ernie and Gail Mills saw a need and provided a refuge for the homeless.

"If it wasn't for Preacher Mills and Mrs. Mills, I don't know if I'd still be here on this earth today. I probably would have backslid, but they showed me a lot of love. That's what kept me going. I never had that before. I didn't want to let them down. Preacher Mills gave me the kind of love I should have gotten from my father, and he also taught me about my heavenly Father," said Holloway.

Others tell equally dramatic stories.

"I'd be dead," or "I would have lost custody of my kids," are common responses to the question of what would have happened to individuals without the help of the Durham Rescue Mission.

"I'd still be strung out on drugs," or "My boyfriend would have kept beating me," or "I'd be on the street somewhere," others responded.

The individual circumstances are innumerable, but their basic needs were the same when they arrived. They needed shelter, food, clothing, and understanding, all of which are abundantly and generously offered at the Mission.

The motto of the Mission is to offer *"a compassionate hand up—not a hand out"* to an often disadvantaged and desperate population.

It isn't pity people receive when they walk through the doors of the Mission, although many who come certainly deserve it. Instead, they are greeted with open arms and a genuine spirit of love.

Some of those who have needed the Mission tell stories of reckless descents into alcohol abuse and drug addiction. Other stories are about living on the fringes of society, while still others are about loss—the loss of jobs, money, homes, friends, families, self respect, and finally any hope of climbing out of the abyss into which they have sunk. The Mission works to restore hope and dignity.

Because they have no other family members to turn to for help or guidance, many Mission residents call the couple "Pop and Momma Mills." Likewise, the surrounding downtown community—long plagued by poverty and inner city strife—often receives assistance from the Mission. Hundreds of needy neighbors attend community dinners at the Mission several times a year. All are welcomed at these neighborhood outreach events intended to lift the spirits of the needy. People get hot meals, a few bags of groceries, clothing, toys and school supplies for their children, anything the Mission can offer that might prevent another family from becoming homeless. At these community events, those attending not only hear about the love of God, but also see it in action.

The story of the Mission is the story of Ernie and Gail Mills. Both exude an infectious enthusiasm and are always ready with a smile or a hug to brighten a miserable day. Their story of joyful service to those who are down and out has touched the hearts of many. It has inspired a family of supporters that goes beyond local borders, extending to the corporate community and individuals far and wide. The Durham Rescue Mission is a place where people with vastly different political views and social agendas come together in friendship to work for a common cause—to help the needy.

Ernie Mills speaks quietly, easily drawing people in with his sincere and humble testimony. But don't let his gentle, easy manner mislead. A steely determination and unbreakable faith have fueled this soft-spoken preacher to overcome insurmountable odds with grace and great humor.

He gives much of the credit for what the Mission has come to mean in the community to his steadfast wife. But they both give all of the glory to God. They are gleefully unapologetic about their real mission—to save lost souls with the Gospel of Jesus Christ. Even skeptics who don't share their strong convictions find the couple endearing and lend support, only fueling the couple's faith. They have faced sometimes seemingly impossible challenges. Yet, with prayer, resilience and personal sacrifice, they persevered, and witnessed how God made things beyond their wildest dreams possible in accomplishing their mission to tell all those who are hurting that God loves them.

The inspiring and triumphant story of how the Mission came to be begins on a tiny tobacco farm in rural eastern North Carolina where Ernie Mills grew up.

Once when Ernie Mills was a boy, he thought it would be entertaining to stand on a boulder in the deep end of an irrigation pond behind the family's farm house. The water looked like it was barely up to his knees, so Ernie tricked his baby brother—who couldn't swim—into wading in the "shallow" end with him.

According to family folklore, the story goes that his parents had to fish the nearly unconscious youngster out with a pole.

High spirited—but never mean spirited—Ernie was brimming with energy. He and his two younger brothers, Jay and Bobby, all had a knack for getting into mischief around the family's tobacco farm, usually with Ernie and Jay conspiring together to taunt younger Bobby. Ernie invariably led the rambunctious childhood cause. The wiry youth never failed to entice his brothers along for whatever misadventure he could dream up. The scrappy farm boys were prone to teasing each other and wrestling furiously at the drop of a hat.

For years, the kids amused themselves in an underground hideout dug down into a giant mound of dirt left from creating an irrigation pond on a neighboring farm.

Plywood pieces created the roof and flap door entrance, which the boys disguised with dirt over the top to keep their hideaway secret. They would lower down a bucket of coal to keep it toasty, running a pipe for a smoke stack up through the roof. The reasons why still elude him, but one day Ernie blocked the flue and door—with little Bobby inside as the coal smoked away.

They got him out before he suffocated, but had refused to open the door until he stopped that hysterical pounding on the roof and screaming to get out. He stopped screaming all right. He was gasping for breath when they carried him out.

Ernie was just curious where all that smoke would go. At least that is the only reason Ernie can surmise about the story which became a notorious family legend. He never meant to accidentally asphyxiate his baby brother. The thought certainly never entered his mind that Bobby could be hurt. It was just a joke among kids, a little childhood prank gone awry, no different than the scuffles that routinely broke out among the rough and tumble trio.

Besides, those lighthearted shenanigans were about the only outlet for an otherwise difficult upbringing on that farm. It was far from a carefree childhood for Ernie and his siblings. They all worked just as hard as they played, if not harder. As much as Ernie was allowed to run barefoot and unfettered in his spare time, he was also expected to get his farming chores done. Indeed, by age 15, young Ernie assumed much of the responsibility for running the farm since he was the oldest son.

Ernie's birthplace in Ayden, NC. Ernie lived here until he was five years old with his parents, who were sharecroppers, and his 3 siblings.

As he was growing up, people called Ernie by his middle name, Charles, so as not to confuse him with his daddy, Ernest. Once grown, at age 19, Ernie decided he wanted to use his first name. After that, the only people who called him Charles were from back home. But, Ernie preferred his first name to honor his father who worked so hard to give him a better life.

His father, Ernest, a poor sharecropper, had to sell one of the hogs he raised just to get enough money for a marriage license. About seven years later, Ernest and Athalene Stocks Mills sold some more hogs to help raise the money to buy their 40-acre farmstead in a place called Frog Level.

Frog Level was located on the outskirts of the eastern North Carolina city of Greenville, then a bustling center for the tobacco trade. Natives smile when they speculate about the history of why the farm road on the southwest edge of town became known as "Frog Level."

"Perhaps it had a lot of frogs and it was level ground," is their simple reply.

In 1949, when the Mills family moved there, Ernie was five years old. At the time, Frog Level was nothing more than a dirt crossroads dotted with tobacco farms, worked mostly by sharecroppers or itinerant farm hands.

Ernie's parents had worked hard to buy a farm and were grateful they no longer had to harvest someone else's crop each year.

The cramped four-room white plank farmhouse had no electricity and no indoor plumbing. A pot bellied coal stove in the living room heated the small house, while kerosene lamps provided the only light at night. Mama cooked on a coal stove. This was definitely a step up from the two-room house where Ernie was born in Ayden, North Carolina. An outhouse and crowded conditions were not considered hardships. It was just life on the farm.

The family grew corn to feed their hogs, and they tried to grow 25 bushels of Irish potatoes each year for the family to eat. That meant potatoes for at least two meals a day. His daddy would kill seven hogs each year to keep the family in country ham and bacon. A typical hearty breakfast consisted of fried pork chops, gravy, and his Mama's homemade cheese-filled biscuits sopped in Grandma's Molasses. They called those mouthwatering delights "cat head" biscuits because Mama made them as big as a cat's head. She cooked up those mounds of flaky crust wrapped around balls of melted cheese to satisfy this hardworking bunch.

They also kept chickens, and Mama sure knew how to fry them up. Of course, Mama would stew just about anything to keep the family fed—from turtles to possums to pigeons. She would even cook up the muskrats the boys trapped for their skins—although she said she would never tell them what they were eating. If they thought it was squirrel or rabbit, they wouldn't turn their noses up at it. The kids all loved Mama's country cooking and thrived on what the farm provided.

Chapter 2
EARLY LESSONS ON HATING THE SIN AND LOVING THE SINNER

*E*rnie was never hungry, but store-bought groceries were a rare luxury because cash was so scarce.

Somehow, there always seemed to be enough money for Daddy to buy some bootleg White Lightning though. In later years, Ernie would drive his father, a chronic alcoholic, to the ABC store because his father was either too sick or too drunk to drive. His father would buy as much liquor as the store would allow, keeping some for himself and planning to bootleg the rest to neighbors and friends. Ernie remembers men coming to the back door all through the night as his dad sold the alcohol by the drink from the bottles he had purchased at the ABC store.

Ernie's only unhappy boyhood memories poured from those inescapable liquor bottles. They lined the pantry and refrigerator shelves, the floor next to the sofa, wherever his father might abandon them in a drunken stupor. The liquor his father perpetually drank was siphoning the life out of him at far too young an age. The amber liquid was drowning his good health.

Paradoxically, despite rarely being sober, his father was always a good provider and, more importantly, a devoted parent

Ernie's dad, Ernest Mills. This is the only visual memory Ernie has of his beloved dad.

whom Ernie loved dearly and remembers compassionately. In hindsight, Ernie recalls those times with gratitude and a profound understanding of his father's role in shaping his life.

"A lot of people who grew up with alcoholics have such a hatred for them because they suffered abuse," Ernie said. "My dad was a very unusual alcoholic. He was a very loving father—very caring. We never went hungry. We were never homeless. He was able to maintain the farm."

The only thing Ernie's father knew how to write was his name. His mother had no education, either, having lost both her parents at just five years old. Shipped around to various aunts and uncles afterwards, Athalene never went to school because she was put to work where she was needed in the fields.

Once married, Athalene knew well how to keep life going on the farm. Ernie loves to impishly share his mama's home-spun cures for the various childhood ailments he and his siblings encountered on the farm.

"Mama's remedy for chicken pox was to take us out to the chicken coop. She'd make us bend down in the threshold of the chicken coop, and she would shoo the chickens out over our heads. It *scared* me to death! But"—Ernie pauses during this oft told story, and continues facetiously—"I don't have the pox today, so it must have worked."

Both his mother and father had led hard lives and weren't prone to any outward show of affection. Ernie never heard "I love you" from his father. Still, he knew his parents were working for something better for their children. From a young age, the boys were expected to harvest the crop while Ernie's sister, Ellen, did the bulk of the household chores and helped her mother.

Back when Ernest first began bootlegging—one of the

early enterprises of this thrifty and industrious farmer—he never drank. He said moonshine was for selling, not drinking. It was only after debilitating arthritis pain began to plague him that he tried liquor to make it better. Instead, it got the better of him.

"My father used alcohol like my husband takes Celebrex," said Ellen, whose married name is Carr. "We didn't have some of these high powered pain killers. We didn't have the knowledge. He knew the alcohol would take the edge off the terrible pain of the gout and arthritis. He didn't know it would make it worse. I never looked at my dad as an alcoholic because he looked out for us. My dad was never abusive. He was a very good father."

Ellen also remembers her father's compassion more than his drinking. She said two of her father's brothers were also chronic alcoholics, but it was her father who was forever bailing them out and helping whoever he could. Ernie, she said, inherited that kindness and concern for others, all the while witnessing the destruction that drinking could do to such a good man.

Their father's feet and hands swelled so much that he couldn't get out in the fields to work or even stand to supervise the workers. The children only had a small inkling that these outward symptoms predicted something much worse to come.

Nicknamed "Keg" because of his barrel shape, Ernie's dad carried 300-pounds on his 5 foot 9 inch frame, his sturdy presence a source of reassurance to the family. When he became practically bedridden in the latter stages of cirrhosis of the liver, as the oldest son, Ernie began to shoulder more and more responsibility on the farm.

"If we eat this winter, then you and the boys gotta bring in the crop," Ernie's father would tell him. The teenager would have to hire the farm hands himself by trekking into Greenville to find day laborers to harvest the tobacco and take the crop to market.

"These were the poorest of the poor," Ernie said of the indigent of the city, who were predominantly black. This was when Ernie first learned compassion for a group of people all but forgotten by society, people who had even less than he did as a boy. Those early management skills working with a dispossessed and all but disenfranchised population would come in handy later in life, although he didn't think about that at the time.

His father would periodically try to stop drinking. The doctors at Pitt County Hospital in Greenville warned him repeatedly he was going to die if he didn't stop. He was referred to Duke University Hospital once for treatment of advanced cirrhosis of the liver. That time he seemed to get the message.

He dried out in the hospital and came home sober, promising it was for good. The family breathed a collective sigh of relief. Young Ernie was able to invite friends over for the first time because he wasn't ashamed that his dad would be drunk.

"I came home one day from (high) school a couple of months later, and Dad was drunk again. I don't believe he could have hurt me any worse than if he threw a knife in me. I can still feel that pain today," said Ernie, his soft-spoken southern drawl full of emotion as if it had been yesterday instead of more than 45 years before.

It was clear Ernie's dad wanted to stop drinking, but he was addicted. He was deeply concerned and did not want to pass it along to his children. "I remember several times with Dad, when the cirrhosis was so bad—I guess I was 15 or 16—he would call me to his bedside. He said, 'Son, look at me. Don't you never drink it. It will do this to you,'" recalled Ernie. "I've always been scared of alcohol. I saw what it was doing to him."

Only two years after the Duke hospitalization, Ernie's father died in 1960 at barely age 40, leaving his wife and children to fend for themselves on the farm. For 17-year-old Ernie, his father's death would leave an indelible mark on his future.

Looking back on more than three decades as a Baptist preacher, Ernie Mills realizes how God used the tragedy of his father's death. The hardships he endured growing up the son of an alcoholic prepared Ernie for God's perfect plan for his life. God used the excruciating boyhood experience of watching the person he loved most lose a brutal battle with alcohol by showing him how to help others. At such a tender age, he could not have known that those early memories would become the foundation for his lifelong ministry.

"I saw that Dad wasn't a living example. But I learned he was a dying example," Ernie said.

How different their lives might have been, he is fond of saying, had someone shared the Gospel of God's love and redemption and shown him that through Christ anything is possible, even victory over alcohol addiction.

Back then, Ernie could not have imagined choosing to spend his life working with alcoholics after liquor killed his father. He couldn't stand the stuff and wanted as far away from it as possible. God, it would seem, had a different plan.

Chapter 3
YOUNG FARMER LEAVES DIRT CROSSROADS FOR THE CROSS

*E*rnie Mills is still embarrassed about his poor spelling and grammar, although some might argue that the understated, down-home way he turns a phrase is a large part of the southern preacher's charm. As a student, however, if someone had predicted the bashful farm boy would grow up to be an evangelical preacher; preparing sermons, inspiring congregations, fundraising in the community and speaking to the media on a regular basis, he

Ernie's first year at college. Students were required to wear suits to church, and Ernie had to get this suit from a "mission barrel" where students donated their "hand-me-downs."

likely would have laughed in his self-deprecating manner.

As his wife Gail likes to remind him, Moses didn't have very good verbal skills, but God helped him do what needed to be done. Ernie doesn't need a surrogate, however, as Moses did with Aaron. On the contrary, Ernie's great public appeal seems to stem directly from that unpolished, unembellished natural delivery that brings a story to life. He may hate to write, but in preaching straight from his heart rather than a script, he routinely stirs many hearts to action.

In school, Ernie excelled in math and science. However, he struggled with his other studies, especially those that involved writing. After high school, he was planning to train to become an electrical engineer. There's not much writing involved with that.

It's no wonder Ernie developed an early dislike of school. Once the family got to Frog Level, his illiterate dad decided it was a good time to send his eldest son off to school with his sister, Ellen. The trouble was the school system saw things differently. Ernie was only five, and you had to be six to enter first grade. His dad put him on the bus anyway and sent him to school.

The school sent him right back home on the bus, but that didn't convince his father. He kept sending him until the school kept him. Despite good grades and learning to read, the school held him back, probably because of his age. After that, he admits, "I just about cheated my way through school any time I could."

He flunked the sixth grade. But after that, a natural aptitude for mathematics inspired him to apply himself to his studies, graduating near the top of his high school class in math and science, although the same could not be said of his classes that involved a lot of reading and writing.

With the farm rented out to a neighbor after his father's death, Ernie was excited about being enrolled in nearby Pitt Community College in Winterville. He had already taken night courses in advanced math and electrical circuitry and planned to start full time in the fall following graduation.

That's when the Rev. Frank Smith came to visit.

Preacher Smith invited Er-

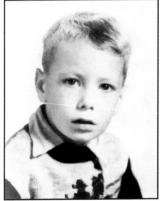

6-year-old Ernie was caught in a "tug-of-war" between his dad and the Pitt County school system.

nie's sister, Ellen and her husband Richard Carr, who were living in a mobile home on the family farm, to a revival at People's Baptist Church in Greenville. Ellen invited Ernie— or rather insisted he come along. It had been years since they attended church, so they weren't quite sure what to expect.

The Rev. Dale Fasenfelt was preaching the revival, and his passionate gospel message brought Ellen and Richard forward to accept Jesus Christ as their savior that morning.

Ernie was so overwhelmed with the conviction of the Holy Spirit; his knees nearly buckled, and he could not remain standing during the invitation. He resisted going forward, though.

"I knew no Christians had a good time," he recalls today, only half facetiously. "I wanted to have a good time in college and sow my wild oats. Then I'd think about becoming a Christian."

When a gentleman approached and offered to go forward with him, Ernie leapt to his feet and shook his head with an emphatic, "no."

"I could see he was under great conviction," recalled Norman Pollard, a deacon in the church who was sitting

Norman Pollard

behind Ernie and had made that offer. Pollard approached the quiet teenager a second time when he saw Ernie was unable to stand once again. Looking back, Ernie said the overpowering burden of sin was what weighed him back down in that pew.

Ernie could no longer resist. He accepted Pollard's second offer to go forward. Then, Pollard led him to a counseling room to answer his questions.

Pollard introduced him first to the book of Romans, which says: "For all have sinned and come short of the glory of God" (Romans 3:23), and "Whosoever shall call upon the name of the Lord shall be saved" (Romans 10:13).

That day—June 7, 1964—19-year-old Ernie Mills became a Christian, changing all his future plans.

"It was an about face. I asked God to forgive my sins and come into my heart and save me," he said.

Pollard took Ernie under his wing, giving him Bible verses to memorize, mentoring him, and taking him along on church visitations to people in the community.

Ernie's heart was so changed by his newfound faith that the Apostle Paul's letter to the Romans spoke right to him. Paul wrote in the epistle about the responsibility of Christians to be bold in sharing the Gospel with everyone.

Soon after that, Pollard's discipleship had Ernie winning souls to the Lord. Within weeks, Ernie said he "felt a heaviness on my heart to share the good news of Jesus Christ with others." Instead of Pitt Community College, he enrolled at Bob Jones University in Greenville, South Carolina, based only on the recommendation of People's Baptist Church Pastor Jack Mosher.

Pollard said he watched in awe as Ernie's life was completely transformed by receiving the Gospel, and he has been equally impressed by the fruit of that dramatic change.

"He has lived such a wonderful life of faith. I am just amazed at how both Ernie and Gail trusted God. And God has honored that and is doing great things through them. God has taken him and used him in a mighty way," Pollard said.

Chapter 4
CONTEMPLATING HIS FUTURE, ASPIRING PREACHER REVISITS HIS PAST
But first, a "Humble" apology.

Getting through that first year at college was no simple feat. The first year, without a car, he jogged the five miles to and from the Cash and Carry Grocery Store, where he worked stocking shelves and unloading trucks. He eventually got in pretty good shape, but wouldn't have been able to make the jog each day that first month if he hadn't tightly wrapped his aching legs from ankle to thigh in Ace bandages.

Most of the money he earned from those odd jobs, and as an electrician's helper during the summer, went to pay his tuition. He could afford to treat himself to only one Coca Cola a week; all the while watching his roommates drink as many as they wanted each day. He would save his Coca Cola for Sunday evenings when sandwiches and a snack were delivered to the dorm rooms because the dining hall was closed.

Money was a stumbling block, but it was nothing compared to the academic hurdles that confronted him at Bob Jones University. One hurdle was being unfamiliar with even basic Bible stories, while most of the other students learned them as children. Perhaps the greatest hurdle was that despite earning a high school diploma, Ernie's college entrance exam score placed him at an eighth grade reading level. This did not serve him well at the demanding university.

One lesson he took to heart during that first grueling year at the university was that he had a confession to make.

"Truly, it was a humbling experience," said Ernie as he recounted the visit he felt compelled to make to a woman aptly named—Mrs. Humbles.

Mrs. Ray Humbles ran the local store in Frog Level. After a year of intense study of the Bible, Ernie thought she couldn't have a more appropriate last name where he was concerned. He would have to be humble to finally tell that sweet old lady the truth.

Ernie was one of many local kids in the rural farming community who would congregate to buy penny candy at Mrs. Humbles' store through the 1950s and 60s. The kindly storekeeper would send the children behind the candy counter to pick out what they wanted of the colorful confections.

"She was always so nice," he said.

It was so easy to take advantage of her kindness, a fact that didn't weigh heavy on his heart until years later. The 20-year-old Ernie paid a visit to Mrs. Humbles in the summer of 1965.

He had spent the previous few months studying his new roadmap of life...The Holy Bible, and it was time to make amends.

Gathering all the humility the young man could muster, Ernie stood before Mrs. Humbles' familiar candy counter once again. This time he wasn't there to buy bubble gum. He was there to make restitution.

"Mrs. Humbles, each time I was behind the counter, picking out a couple pieces of candy, I was stealing a pack of cigarettes and then paying you only for the candy. I want to pay you for what I stole," Ernie said.

"She started crying and I started crying. It's clearing one's conscience. I really believe if you've wronged anybody, you ought to make it right."

The sincere, understated way he tells the story is a hallmark of his ministry, as are the powerful emotions he evokes.

The confession taught him a lasting lesson and lifted a lingering burden. Back at school, however, the mountain of academic pressure was still weighing heavily on him.

"I'm not the sharpest knife in the drawer," declares the humble preacher, although there are many who would dispute that. "I couldn't cut the mustard in college. I was failing more grades than I passed."

After a year and a half at school, he transferred what credits he had earned to the university's Institute for Christian Service, a course of study with a more practical application of theological values than the rugged academics he faced at first. While still challenged, Ernie was able to graduate.

In the weeks preparing for graduation, he was reading, "In His Steps," the 1896 novel by Charles Monroe Sheldon who asked the famous question, "What would Jesus do?" People in the book dedicate themselves to serving others and helping the poor. Characters in the book learn through prayer to give up drinking, to become friends of Christ, and to the needy.

Ernie's childhood memories came flooding back. Contemplating his future, he kept recalling his past. He thought of his drunken dad, and could not remember anyone trying to help him or witness to him about the Lord.

"God just laid the alcoholic firmly on my chest. Images of my dad kept coming back to me, and that nobody would help him. At that time, places to help them were few and far between. I felt like that was the ministry God would have me do. My childhood experiences had taught me to hate alcohol, but God just gave me a love for the alcoholic and a desire to help them. I just share that love, that burden. I just share that with other people. It's not Ernie Mills. It's the Lord that does it."

When he went to tell the dean of ministerial students he was looking for a way to help alcoholics, he was greeted with a knowing smile. Ernie had most assuredly discerned the correct message. Why, only the previous week, said Dean Gilbert Stenholm, he'd had a visit from the Rev. Neal Wilcox.

Wilcox, a Bob Jones University alumnus, had founded a rescue mission for alcoholics in Winston-Salem the pervious year. He was in need of an assistant with a heart for helping homeless alcoholics.

Ernie graduated in 1968 with a three-year Bible certificate in Christian Service. He was ordained on June 7, 1968 back at People's Baptist Church in Greenville, exactly four years to the day that he was saved in the same church. From there, he went right to work at the Winston-Salem Rescue Mission.

Chapter 5

A "NATURAL TEAM" AND A MATCH MADE IN HEAVEN

When Neal Wilcox started the Winston-Salem Rescue Mission in July of 1967, he didn't know the city was about to erupt into race riots. All he knew was that he was needed so he moved into the apartment on the second floor of the Mission building to begin his ministry.

"It meant I'd have to live on Skid Row, in an undesirable section of town that had been deteriorating for a while," Wilcox said.

It also meant his wife would be living there, with all the troubled men they were trying to help sleeping downstairs each night. Only four months later, the violent rioting started, and as a white couple, they feared the hundreds of rioting black protestors would misdirect their anger at them. In fact, during one of the worst nights, when vandals were looting and destroying buildings in their path, they spared the mission but burned buildings on either side.

That very night, before the mayhem, a guest preacher in the mission's chapel service took his text from Exodus 12:13. It is the story of the Passover, God's promise to Moses to spare the Israelites' first born children among those faithful families who painted their door posts with the blood of the lamb. That night, Wilcox truly saw the protecting hand of God as the rioters passed over the Mission.

Those were tumultuous times, but Wilcox stayed with his new ministry. Within a year, the Mission was serving 25 men a night. With an around-the-clock-schedule, a baby on the way, and more social turmoil sparked by the assassination of Martin Luther King Jr., Wilcox realized he needed help. He had proven his heart was in the Mission and that he was there to stay, but he needed to move his wife and newborn baby.

"We were pretty much a natural team," Wilcox said about his new assistant, Ernie Mills.

Ernie, with mentor, Neal Wilcox, taking a break during a conference in Arizona to visit a "dude ranch." They just had to try on those cowboy hats!

"We both wanted to do what God wanted us to do. I'm from Kinston, which is 28 miles from Greenville, so we spoke the same dialect," Wilcox quipped. "We were from the same area and graduated from the same college."

The difference was that Ernie grew up watching his father drink himself to death, and Wilcox, who never knew his father, was raised by his Christian grandparents who did not drink.

The Mission paid for the new assistant by selling recycled newspapers for a penny a pound. Donations of clothing and other items from churches and the community also started piling up faster than the Mission could use them.

With a Scotch, Irish and Jewish heritage, Wilcox likes to joke; he couldn't stand anything not being used. He started a store, selling the donated items to support the Mission. Nearly four decades later, the endeavor grew to provide 60 percent of the Mission's income.

The 5½ years Ernie spent at the Winston-Salem Rescue Mission would provide a crucial foundation for his future ministry—and not just because of the hands-on training and

Gail's high school picture. When Ernie set his eyes on Gail, he says his life was changed forever!

mentoring he got from Wilcox.

Ernie smiles when he tells the story of the first time he set eyes on his future wife. It was 1968 just before a church service at the Winston-Salem Rescue Mission. Ernie always says he was looking out over the congregation of drunks, and "there she sat." Gail Gerrey certainly wasn't one of the drunks, but to this day she smiles patiently as her husband tells his favorite yarn about their first encounter. She was there volunteering with her church youth group.

Gail grew up poor in a family where both her mother and father worked to eek out a living. Ted Gerrey, Gail's father, sold and serviced vending machines and jukeboxes, while her mother, Audrey, worked in a hosiery mill. Her father died after a swift and devastating bout with spinal meningitis. His sudden death left Gail, her mother and her two brothers, Jerry, the oldest child, and Teddy, the youngest, in shock and devastation.

Shortly after her father died, the local dry cleaning service driver, old Mr. Venerable, who was a Christian, invited her family to church. The salvation message went straight to Gail's broken heart, and, at age 13, the seventh grader became a Christian.

She was faithful to church during her high school years in Winston-Salem and stayed with the youth group even after she graduated. She was 19 the night she met Ernie. The youth choir was there early so before the service, Gail was sitting in the front pew of the chapel reading her Bible.

Ernie approached her and asked what she was reading.

"I'm reading a love story," she replied playfully.

Ernie guessed First Corinthians 13, the famous "love chapter" of the Bible so often read at wedding ceremonies as a reminder that love is patient and kind, and to exercise God's gifts in the spirit of love.

"No," answered Gail with a grin. She was reading her favorite Bible story, the book of Ruth, words from which are also often included in modern Christian wedding ceremonies. "For whither thou goest, I will go," the biblical Ruth tells her mother-in-law Naomi after tragedy strikes and Ruth's husband dies. Her loyalty to her mother-in-law is rewarded. The name Ruth means "friendship," an exemplification of God's love and care.

Looking back, Gail smiles and opens her arms in mock melodrama at her first encounter with Ernie. "I should have said, 'and here's my Boaz,'" whom Ruth marries after returning to Bethlehem with Naomi.

But, of course, the demure teen did nothing of the sort. They both nodded and went on with preparations for the service. Afterward, Ernie gave the visiting church group a tour. At one point, Ernie saw his chance to find out a little bit more about the girl he had his eye on. He took one of Gail's friends aside to ask her if Gail was dating anyone.

He was deflated when the girlfriend told Ernie she was.

"That put a cool on that," Ernie said.

The youth group left, and Gail drove two of her friends to McDonald's for hamburgers.

"My friend Shandra said, 'You would die if you knew what that boy at the Mission asked me. I told him you were dating my brother, Junior."

Appalled, Gail said, "I took her right to a phone booth

August 30, 1969, Ernie and Gail joined together in marriage and ministry of caring for the least, the last, and the lost.

and made her call Ernie to tell him I wasn't dating Junior. Junior just picked me up for church. She gave Ernie my phone number, and when I got home the phone was ringing."

"It was on!" said Ernie, cheerfully slapping a knee at the memory of how they began dating. It didn't take long to know they were meant for each other, but Ernie refused to "rob the cradle" and marry a teenager. Gail turned 20 on July 31. The couple was married August 30, 1969 at Crestview Baptist Church in Winston-Salem.

Ernie's mischievous tone about their dating days changes quickly to reverence as he talks about their marriage.

"I think it was the Lord's will for us to be a couple," he said after more than three and a half decades of marriage. Still, there were those who had their doubts in the beginning.

"The only place we had to live when we got married was in the apartment on the second floor of the Winston-Salem Rescue Mission on Skid Row. I remember my mother's fears," Gail said, which weren't misplaced, because the neighborhood had not improved significantly since the rioting.

"But I always felt like a queen living at the Mission. There was a fenced-in parking lot across from the mission, and Ernie would always be waiting there to walk me across the street when I got home from work. If he couldn't be there, one of the residents would be there to make sure I got upstairs safely."

She also credits her husband's thrift with allowing them to accomplish their goals.

"When we got married, I was working at McLean Trucking Company and making four times what he was making. Ernie had money in the bank and I was in debt. He was making $40 a week, and he said we were going to live on his salary. We wanted children, and if we got used to living on both of our incomes, I wouldn't be able to stay home with them."

Gail's paycheck was deposited directly in the bank for their future plans.

Chapter 6
A WING, A PRAYER... AND TWO BARRELS OF HEATING OIL

*I*t just wasn't sensible.

Ernie could find no compelling reason to leave his job at the Winston-Salem Rescue Mission, he told himself in 1973. He didn't want to leave. He was doing work he loved and felt he was called by God to do. He was needed there. He was happily married, and his 1½-year-old son Ernie, Jr., was thriving.

After living above the Winston-Salem Rescue Mission for about a year, the couple bought a 14-acre parcel of land and settled into a mobile home they were buying. Ernie was gradually clearing the underbrush and turning the land into an attractive lot. Why give up a perfectly good job when so many people were being laid off? For months he wrestled with the decision.

There simply was no earthly reason to go.

No earthly reason, perhaps. But ultimately he could not ignore the fact that he had a higher calling. He knew in his heart God wanted him in Durham.

Durham, one tip of what was known as The Triangle— along with Raleigh and Chapel Hill, North Carolina—was significant in the Revolutionary and Civil wars, and full of historic antebellum plantations. It boasted well-established cotton, hosiery, and tobacco mills. At the same time, it was on the cutting edge of technology with the innovative and growing Research Triangle Park.

Durham became known as the "Bull City" because of the famous Bull Durham Tobacco trademark that had even sparked the phrase "bullpen" because of the Bull Durham ad painted behind the New York Yankees' dugout. Otherwise, to Ernie, it was just home to Duke University Hospital. That's where his father had gone as a last hope to get treatment for advanced cirrhosis of the liver.

Ernie knew the Veterans Administration Hospital was located there. That made Durham a strategic location for veterans, many of whom abused drugs or were post traumatic from the Vietnam War. Some families rejected them as they failed to reintegrate back into society following their service. Alcoholism was getting even more common for servicemen. Ernie really couldn't say why Durham weighed so heavily on his heart. All he knew was he was supposed to start a mission there.

Still, 1973 was not an auspicious time to go looking for money in any community across the nation. Aside from the constant news of layoffs and economic downturns, the public was distracted by the ever-widening Watergate scandal. Rumblings of a presidential impeachment were circulating. The economy was slipping as interest rates were skyrocketing.

Then, by year's-end, OPEC's oil embargo against the United States, Europe and Japan would strain fuel supplies everywhere, escalating electricity and energy costs. That meant church offerings were down because of layoffs.

Furthermore, Ernie didn't know a soul in Durham. He logically reasoned to himself that it just wasn't feasible to go and try to start a mission there when no one ever had before. Nobody was asking him to do it. How could he find sponsors to finance a rescue mission in Durham? The list of obstacles was too overwhelming and the odds against success too heavy to uproot his family and risk their security, he decided.

That sensible approach worked about as well as Jonah sailing off to Tarshish to avoid the Lord's command to pronounce God's judgment against the wicked people of Nineveh. After a couple of months of agonizing over the decision, he surrendered. He put the land up for sale—but, his thriftiness wouldn't allow him to list it with an agent because he didn't want to pay a commission. Also, he furtively hoped, perhaps it would delay any interest in the land.

The property sold within a week.

"It's like the Lord said, 'You fought with me now for two months. It's time to get moving,'" Ernie recalled.

Still, with the economy sliding ever downward, they had to agree to finance the sale of the land themselves because banks wouldn't approve the loan. They also agreed (inexplicably, as Gail reflects back on their inexperience) to taking single annual payments rather than monthly installments from the buyer. Through this time, they trusted the Lord, the couple says. But they also clung tightly to their bank balance for security.

Ernie Junior burst into tears when he saw the family's 10-by-55-foot aluminum mobile home being towed from its cinderblock foundation on that sunny November day in 1973. The family followed behind the trailer as they headed up Interstate 85 North to Durham. Gail drove Ernie Junior in the family car, and Ernie drove a van they bought from the Winston-Salem Rescue Mission. In the back, he had two 55-gallon drums of heating oil, since he was aware no oil companies were accepting new customers during the embargo.

"We were fearful we would not be able to buy heating oil when we got to Durham, so we thought we had to have that oil to keep us from freezing that first winter," Gail said.

"Our faith was so small," she smiles.

It wasn't long before they did find a willing oil distributor after all. His name, appropriately enough, was Don Christian. He was a member of Calvary Baptist Church in Durham. While he wasn't taking on new customers, he made an exception for the young missionaries.

Ernie felt deep in his heart that Durham was where they ought to be, but had no idea how he would accomplish the task at hand. That first year, they didn't have a building. They only had a few people donate to their unproven ministry.

When they arrived in Durham, the couple made the rounds to local churches, looking for spiritual and financial support. They found some like-minded pastors who offered their support. One day, they stopped by Wayside Baptist Church in Hillsborough, North Carolina, where they met Pastor Larry Carter as he was getting out of his car.

They told him why they'd come to the area, and Pastor Carter suddenly threw his arms around Ernie in a bear hug. He exclaimed: "You're an answer to prayer! You're the one we've been waiting for!"

Carter had witnessed the growing need for a mission in the community because hospitals refused to admit alcoholics just for being drunk. He was frustrated by not having a place to take alcoholics and homeless men where they could get real help and counseling, but had been unsuccessful finding enough support to get a mission started.

He tried to enlist civic leaders in Hillsborough and the nearby Durham area to help with the cause.

Larry Carter (left) and H. L. Mickle (front right) supported the Durham Rescue Mission from the very beginning.

Some community leaders set up a meeting to discuss possible plans for a shelter for the homeless and asked Carter to speak to their group.

They selected their favorite meeting place—the back room of the local ABC liquor store. Carter drove up to the store at the appointed hour, but the Baptist minister just couldn't bring himself to get out of the car, let alone step inside or be seen stepping into the liquor store. He simply drove away, and the dream of a mission for homeless alcoholics languished.

He recounted the story to Ernie to explain his enthusiastic greeting in the church parking lot when they first met, and why he immediately offered his assistance in getting the Durham Rescue Mission started. He gave his valuable endorsement to the newcomers in the community where he was well-known and loved, and naturally, Carter became one of the first board members for the Mission.

From the beginning, he was impressed with what the Durham Rescue Mission accomplished and marvels at how steadfast the Mills have been in their ministry. "Ernie's doing something that most pastors can't do," said Carter, who served as pastor of Wayside Baptist Church for 32 years. He retired in 1997 from the church he founded.

Without encouragement from people like Rev. Carter, Ernie and Gail might not have stuck it out that first, difficult year in Durham when their mission was still a dream.

*E*rnie didn't have any illusions about how difficult it would be to run a mission, but he was not prepared for the ways God would test him. With no income and no health insurance, their second child, Bethany, was born six weeks premature at 4 pounds, 2 ounces on June 27, 1974 at Watts Hospital in Durham.

Tiny Bethany struggled for her very life for the first 72 hours, but, just 3 months later, she was a happy, healthy, and beautiful little girl!

Doctors explained that she suffered from Highland Membrane Disease, a condition they likened to the infant's lungs being cast in cement. Doctors told the heartbroken parents that if little Bethany lived through the first 72 hours, her chances of survival would be greatly increased.

But, within hours, her condition deteriorated rapidly. The tiny baby was rushed by ambulance to the prestigious—and expensive—Duke University Hospital's pediatric intensive care unit for specialized care.

After a week at Duke, she was breathing better, and was able to go back to the county hospital where she had been born. She would remain there in an incubator for another two weeks.

Ernie was supposed to go to a meeting of pastors in

Kinston, near Greenville, but was burdened about leaving the family while Bethany was still in the hospital. His heart was also heavy as he contemplated the exorbitant medical bills he would be facing without any insurance.

When he had originally scheduled the meeting, he thought all he would be concerned about was raising the badly needed funds to open the Mission, not about whether his newborn daughter would live. Since Bethany was no longer in critical condition, Gail encouraged Ernie to go. She reminded him it was critical for him to meet with these pastors. He had logged many miles appealing to remote churches in hopes of finding sponsors, but had accumulated precious few donations. He knew the conference was a good place to spark interest in the Mission and that he must go. With Gail on strict orders from her doctor not to overdo, Ernie took Ernie Junior with him to the conference.

Ernie wasn't in a sociable mood, to say the least. Raising support was the last thing on his mind. His heart ached not knowing if his child would live and from having to leave Gail alone. He didn't want to be at the conference. He wanted to be at home praying with his wife for their precious baby girl.

The Rev. Bobby Thomas of Calvary Baptist Church in Greenville, NC, preached from Psalms 145. Verse 3 hit Ernie hard. It says: "Great is the Lord and greatly to be praised."

"There weren't much praise in my heart," Ernie sadly realized.

When the pastors headed for dinner, a pastor's wife took care of Ernie Junior while Ernie quietly slipped into an empty Sunday school classroom to pray. He read Psalms 145 over and over again and found himself encouraged by God's Word. He returned to the sanctuary for the afternoon service.

"I remember I could hear the Liberty Trio singing 'Because He Lives, I Can Face Tomorrow.'"

Tears came to Ernie's eyes as the trio sang the second stanza, "How sweet to hold our newborn baby, and feel the pride and joy he brings."

The young Mills family struggled to get the mission going.

"I had never held my baby," Ernie said. "She was in an incubator."

The chorus of the song gave him hope, as it reminded him that no matter what happened, he could face tomorrow, "Because He lives."

When the other pastors heard about his predicament, they took up a special offering to help with the overwhelming medical bills. One of them, a retired pastor, didn't have any money to give so he humbly took off his watch and placed it in the offering plate.

Ernie returned to Durham with a renewed spirit and several promises of support. The exorbitant medical bills were paid within three months because of the kindness of friends who sent financial help. Bethany thrived, proving all the dire predictions wrong.

Their homeless shelter, however, was still homeless. With the economy on the skids, no banks would loan money to finance a homeless shelter in the most blighted area of town.

Ernie and Gail did have some people pulling for them. One of the most helpful and most colorful supporters they met soon after moving to Durham was the Rev. Harold Lee Mickle. A World War II Marine drill sergeant, Mickle main-

Preacher Mickle was instrumental in getting the Durham Rescue Mission "up and running"!

tained that commanding, gruff military voice that Gail first found intimidating and later endearing. She soon discovered that behind the decisive exterior beat a loving, tender heart. He would become like a father to Ernie and Gail.

Raised in the foothills of North Carolina, Mickle had a grit forged in war and from hard scrabble beginnings. He would often tell that he was so poor he had to move his young family into a one-room 14-by-14 foot chicken house on a relative's property. It had become too crowded staying with his wife's sister's family. With one child and another on the way, he had few choices after losing a trucking business early in his career. Remodeling a rent-free chicken coop seemed his best option. With a lot of hard work, he rebounded from those hard days.

He never cared much about religion in his youth. He did respect his wife, Virginia, for her newfound faith when she accepted Christ as her savior in 1949 while listening to the Rev. Harold Sightler preach on the Bright Spot Hour radio broadcast. That night she wrote a letter to her husband telling him she wanted him to be a Christian, too. Deeply touched by her conviction and the courageous change that overcame his frail wife, Mickle promised he would—one day. At the urging of his devout sister-in-law and his wife, he reluctantly relented and attended a church service. He said yes mostly because he loved music. But, he also hoped he would stop being pestered about going to church. He pulled out his one suit from between the mattress and box spring, where he kept it pressed. His tie, he always loved to recount, was nothing more than a string knotted around his collar. He may have dressed up for the occasion, but his expectations were not high.

That night, much to his surprise, he became a Christian, and it wasn't long before he knew why God had given him that strong voice and personality.

Shortly after being saved, he felt called to preach and he told Virginia so. He told his pastor, too, who then invited him to preach on the following Sunday. Virginia was overwhelmed about the idea of giving up their newfound job security despite her strong Christian beliefs.

"I talked to the Lord, like I was talking to a person," she recalled. "Let one precious soul be saved during his sermon, and I'll be satisfied that he is called to preach."

Five people came forward.

Mickle started night classes at Piedmont Bible College, (now Piedmont Baptist College) in Winston-Salem. He was ordained in 1955; the same year he founded The Old Fashioned Tabernacle Independent Baptist Church in Durham, and was pastor there for 30 years.

Preacher Mickle had a captivating charisma and was known for his trademark wit. One vivid memory was how he would often introduce himself at a gathering of preachers. In his deep southern drawl, he would intone: "I'm H. L. Mickle. Bless God! The H. L. stands for hard headed and long winded."

Mickle had taken Ernie under his wing in the early days, even before there was a mission, introducing him around the community and garnering support.

"He could see they were so sacrificial," said Virginia, who family and friends would come to call "Nannie Mickle"

"Preacher and Nannie Mickle"—as many call them. as Preacher Mickle helped guide Ernie, so did Mrs. Mickle love and minister to Gail and the children.

because she became a surrogate grandmother to so many.

Virginia and Harold Mickle were married 58 years when he died of a heart attack at age 85 in 2002. Virginia told Ernie that she heard the loudest clap of thunder when Preacher Mickle slumped over and fell to the ground.

"Nannie Mickle," replied Ernie. "That wasn't thunder. That was Preacher Mickle breaking the sound barrier on his way to heaven!"

Mickle was a well-respected man in the community. When he suggested in his commanding way that someone, "ought to help this boy," they generally didn't require any further recommendation.

Mickle became the president of the first Board of Directors of the Durham Rescue Mission, his unceasing encouragement was a source of optimism for the couple who encountered countless obstacles along the way. His faith in them echoed his strong faith in God. He knew their vision would become reality and that they would find a place to have their mission.

Sure enough, Preacher Mickle was right. One day, after searching for nearly a year, Ernie noticed an abandoned house at 1301 East Main Street in Durham. Vagrants had taken up residence without invitation, and Ernie realized that was the perfect location for the Mission.

This is where it all began— 1301 E. Main St.

No one wanted that dilapidated house, not even the owner. Perhaps that is what drew Ernie to it as a place to house homeless men, who were also in a way discarded by society.

Rehabilitating the rickety structure, however, would prove as challenging as overcoming addiction. There was very little holding the flimsy two-story structure up. It was a flop house for vagrants since the owner had abandoned it a few years before. It had fallen into disrepair from top to bottom. The roof leaked; the plaster was falling off the walls and the foundation was sagging.

The drunks who habitually broke in had routinely kicked in the doors and punched holes in the walls where they carelessly threw their empty booze bottles.

In the 1970s, the declining neighborhood, plus skyrocketing interest rates, equaled a prohibitive real estate market for Ernie's plans. Banks routinely "red-lined" such areas, Ernie said. They would use red ink to circle areas of their maps as no-loan zones. Ernie asked for a loan on the ramshackle house in one of those areas, no less to be used by a faith-based mission, funded only through donations, and to serve penniless drunken derelicts. Loan officers all but laughed at his request.

Ultimately, Ernie had to finance the mortgage through selling church bonds. Selling the church bonds was an uncertain path, too. The Mission Board of Directors set the interest rate for the bonds at 7 percent. Another church, which wanted a new building across town, was simultaneously selling bonds at a 10-percent return. The board knew the Mission could not compete with that high rate of return.

Ernie had only collected a scant $500 in donations that first year to start a Mission, and it occurred to him that if he wanted people to purchase bonds at a lower rate than they could get across town, he had to make his own sacrifice.

He felt God wanted him to donate the money they had in savings to help buy the house.

Ernie knew Gail wouldn't like it. It would mean going without a monetary safety net. He knew he had to ask her, and he also knew it had to be a joint decision. The request: "almost tore her out of her frame," Ernie said.

It did take some time for Gail to get used to the idea. That dwindling bank balance was all the security she had to keep the family fed. She struggled and prayed and cried, "God, if we starve to death, it will be your fault!" She also knew her husband was right. Grief stricken, she ever so hesitantly agreed, taking all but $100 out of the bank for a down payment to purchase the first house.

"We had given *everything*!" Gail said, chuckling now at how small she says her faith was back then. "It was from that point on that God started opening doors for the Mission. I had to come to the point that my trust was in God. It wasn't in that savings account. God used that to show us that He would provide for our needs. I don't know why I kept that $100."

One of those open doors was the fact that Ernie and the board were able to sell enough bonds to buy the house, despite the competition across town. Ironically, the Mission's bond holders got paid off early while that other church with the promise of big profits disbanded its membership and closed down. Their investors lost all their money.

Without a loan, though, the Mission had no money for the numerous urgently needed repairs. This presented a huge problem because city officials were about to condemn the decrepit building. Indeed, one of the first visitors to the Mission was an angry building inspector.

"I've been trying to find the owners for two years," shouted the perturbed public servant who pounded on the fragile front door. He needn't have used force. The flimsy front door swung open because it could not be fastened shut. The door jambs were long ago broken off by vandals. The building inspector abruptly listed all the shortcomings of the structure and impressed upon the fledgling pastor and new property owner that the problems had to be fixed to bring it up to city code.

"I said, 'O-Okay,'" Ernie said with a smile at his meek reply, intimidated by the boisterous inspector. It was a daunting task before him, but he persevered.

One man's trash...

Cold weather set in that November in 1974, and Ernie still had no way to heat the Mission. Although the house had pipes for gas heat, there wasn't a heater.

"I'll never forget the first guy that came," remembered Gail. "We were thrilled. But we had that drafty two-story house, with no heater. To make things worse, the water heater leaked like a sifter so we had no hot water for him either. In the morning, there was only cold cereal to eat."

The homeless man's teeth were chattering as he tried to eat. He shivered and said, "I appreciate what you are trying to do, but I've got to get some place warm," Gail said. "We were crushed."

With mounting frustration, Ernie put his energy into the enormous task of cleaning out the years of accumulated beer, wine, and liquor bottles that had been carelessly tossed into holes in the old walls. This was no small task as the holes had grown with every fist gone astray or body slammed up against a wall during the many brawls that broke out among the vagrants who camped there.

"You've heard of fiberglass insulation," Ernie tells the story now, flashing his trademark grin. "Well, we had just plain old glass insulation."

At the time it wasn't amusing at all. Fuming hotter than his exhaust pipe, Ernie loaded the bed of the pickup truck with the bottles and headed for the dump.

"I'm a preacher, but I was mad. Liquor killed my dad. I was discouraged and I was mad."

At the landfill, wearing heavy work boots, Ernie opened the tailgate and vented his frustrations by kicking the offending bottles out of the truck onto the trash heap. He purposely tried to break as many as possible.

His outburst stopped suddenly when, atop that trash pile, he beheld a shiny gas space heater. Not buried, the heater was there in plain sight above all that trash, with the sun glinting off of its sleek, metal frame, looking just like an answered prayer.

"I bet God put that there just for me," he said, at last recognizing the reason for his disagreeable trip to the dump. "All things work together for good," he said, quoting Romans 8:28.

He called a friend from nearby Mebane. James Florence, the son of Rev. James "Buster" Florence, worked at a Mebane gas company, and he came to Durham to check out Ernie's discarded find. He told Ernie the heater was in perfect working condition and that his company still sold that very model for $300. The Mission now had a way to keep warm. With that problem solved, they now needed hot water.

One day, Jerry Bridges from the local gas company, pulled up in a truck and asked them where they wanted their brand new gas water heater installed. Ernie rushed over to tell the technician he must have the wrong address because the Mission couldn't afford it. "No charge," said Bridges.

They never discovered the name of the Good Samaritan who anonymously donated the much appreciated gift. After hooking it up, however, they discovered the cast iron water pipes were corroded. Deposits clogged the ancient pipes like cholesterol buildup in an artery. Just a trickle of water would come out of the tap when it was turned on full force.

With no money to hire professionals to do the job, Ernie set about learning how to replace the pipes with help from a local plumber and friend, Buddy Malone. He told Ernie he was too busy to re-pipe the house, but he could teach Ernie what needed to be done. Ernie learned quickly how to solder and sweat the joints and ran the pipes through the house. The first time he turned on the new plumbing, there were only two leaks. Not bad for a novice.

With the help of the Mission residents, Ernie began to patch the old house with the materials that came his way. A Hillsborough real estate developer, Raymond Outlaw, gave the Mission two 55-gallon barrels of paint. One was cream and the other was a trendy 1970's avocado green. Because there was no money to patch the walls properly, the rag-tag crew began painting around the gaping holes.

"One of the men said, 'Preacher, I've always been taught that you're supposed to build the house before you paint it.'" Even with the holes, the paint job vastly improved the look of the house, Ernie said.

With the problems inside the house temporarily taken care of, he turned his attention outside. The holes in the roof were a priority on the building inspector's checklist of repairs. Working on that roof brought back blistering boyhood memories of summers patching tobacco barn roofs. His father was too unsteady from drinking, and in too much pain from arthritis, to climb the ladder. Instead, he sent young Ernie up on top of the hot tin roofs with a bucket of black tar cement each June. The technique that kept the moisture out of the tobacco barns worked just as well at keeping the rain out of his new Mission, and it was good to learn that there was a reason for all that hard childhood labor.

Another not-so-fond memory of the early days at the Mission was meal planning, which Ernie, only in later years could look back on with amusement. He had promised the men three meals a day but didn't have money to buy groceries. He walked to local grocery stores and asked if the owners would donate their dented cans. One of them told him to come back with a truck because he had a whole load to give him. To Ernie's dismay, when he got back to the store, the shop keeper had peeled all the labels off of the dented cans for some inexplicable reason. As grateful as he was for the donation, it made meal planning adventurous. They ate a lot of soup during that period.

For breakfast, they had Pink Panther Corn Flakes with powdered milk. Apparently the public wasn't ready for the sugar coated flakes that turned their breakfast milk pink. Neal Wilcox from the Winston-Salem Rescue Mission had an abundance of boxes of the "Edsel of cereals," as Ernie referred to them. Wilcox shared them generously with the struggling new Mission. The cereal was good and semi-nutritious, but it just wasn't what everyone wanted to eat seven days a week, especially with powdered milk. Ernie asked the Lord for some better food.

Ernie decided to go door to door in the surrounding area to ask residents with large vacant lots by their homes if the Mission could grow gardens there. One of the people who said yes was "Old Mr. Tilley." When Ernie approached him, he was standing out by his well drinking water out of a dipper because he didn't have indoor plumbing. Ernie asked him if he minded if he tended his land as a garden spot for the Mission. The friendly southern farmer replied: "Why sure, sonny. And you can use my mule to plow it with, too."

Once again, the skills learned on his father's farm were put to good and grateful use. His boyhood memories of splitting out tobacco middles as he walked behind a mule and a cotton plow with 12-inch sweeps were more pleasant than the rooftop repairs. Even though it was hot in June when he would do the work, he remembers the cool dirt the plow turned up being refreshing on his bare feet. During the summer, he went barefoot because he only got one pair of new shoes each year. That was always in the fall when school started. If he wore a hole in those shoes, his father would fill it with cardboard until it was hot enough to go without shoes.

That first year, with his farming skills, he soon had a bountiful harvest of okra, tomatoes, beans, corn, peas, onions, potatoes and cucumbers coming in for the mission. The problem was that the old ice cream box freezer that the Rev. James Florence had donated was broken for the third and final time; there was just no fixing it again.

Ernie told Gail that he didn't believe God had provided the land and the seed only to have the harvest wilt with no place to preserve it. One day, as he and Gail drove back to the Mission from checking on the garden, they were met by the sight of cheering residents practically dancing around the driveway. Another anonymous donor, this one from Rocky Mount, North Carolina, had Montgomery Wards Department Store deliver a brand new 21-cubic foot upright freezer.

The men had been praying for a freezer, and now they had seen God answer a prayer, Ernie said. The Mission had never had a new kitchen appliance. Now they had a new freezer, most appropriately painted a fashionable (for the 1970s) shade of avocado green—"To match our green walls," smiled Ernie. It made quite a contrast to the old refrigerator that still served them well, but was brush painted neon pink—a little out of place in the all-men's mission.

By this time, the Mission was serving about six or seven men, with a capacity of sleeping 12 in the house. They accepted any man who was homeless, and most of them had drinking problems. Drugs were just beginning to infiltrate Durham during the early years of the Mission.

Ernie held chapel in the front room of the Mission. Someone had donated some old wooden theater seats, where the men sat for the services in the lopsided parlor. The memory of the many sweet services he held there brought to mind another "unique" quality of that first house.

"Most modern churches are built with a sloping floor so the congregation can see. Ours was the same way, although not by design but because of the sinking and sagging of the house."

Ernie is famous for his amusing one-liners. One of his earliest slogans at the Mission was, "If your clothes are no longer becoming to you, we would like them to be coming to us." They were grateful for what they had and cheerful because they were about the business of sharing the Gospel in hopes of saving lost souls.

Chapter 9
A PITIFUL PARSONAGE

The young Mills family moved into their "new home" at 106 N. Holman St. located in a crime-ridden Northeast Central Durham neighborhood.

lthough the Mission was shaping up, from a practical standpoint, the tally in the ledger books may not have looked so bright. When Gail prepared their taxes that first year of operation, she came out with a negative number for the couple's personal income. In a rush to meet the deadline, she sent the taxes off as they were. After all, they had lived off their savings, and even used most of it to help purchase the Mission's first house. If their charitable deductions were more than their income, then their income was negative, right?

The Internal Revenue Service quickly notified them they would be audited and explained that their adjusted gross income on their tax return could not be a negative number. It seemed simple arithmetic when she initially added up the figures, Gail ruefully smiles. The matter got resolved smoothly, which is more than she could say for their living quarters at the time.

In 1974 the Durham Rescue Mission purchased its first house at 1301 East Main Street, and also rented a house at 106 North Holman Street, directly behind the Mission. This would become the Mission's first parsonage for Ernie and the family.

The smaller house was not abandoned because it had been consistently rented. However, the condition was little better than what they found at the Mission house. The rental house had six big rooms with a common hallway, which was used to divide it into two apartments. The previous renters kept dogs, and Gail suspected from the stench inside the house that they never let the dogs out.

"The house just reeked and the roaches were horrible. The house smelled so bad; I took a bucket and filled it with water and a whole bottle of Pine Sol. I left the room I was in to check on Bethany, our four-month-old daughter, and a few minutes later when I came back, there were roaches floating on top of that water," she said. That was not the worst of it.

When they first moved to Durham, Ernie worked for Clegg's Pest Control until his speaking engagements became too demanding and he started working for the Mission full time. His former employer and friend, the Rev. Ralph Clegg, knew about the infestation of roaches at the parsonage, so he sent an employee over to exterminate.

"When he sprayed, you could hear the dead roaches hitting the floor. It sounded just like popcorn popping. The next day, there were hundreds of dead roaches in the bottom of the bathtub," Gail said.

"Oh!" exclaimed long-time friend Virginia Mickle, who was there that day to help Gail clean the house, "I can still hear those roaches." Gail remembers her good friend telling her years later that when she got home from helping her clean, she threw away her clothes.

Throughout the house, there were layers of worn linoleum. She decided to have it all pulled up because it would be a hiding place for the bugs to breed. When it came up, she realized there was only sub-flooring underneath.

"I actually pulled a water hose through the window into the house to rinse the walls after I had scrubbed them. I never had to mop one drop of water because it all leaked out through the sub-flooring. You could see straight through the cracks in the floor to the ground. The house was so drafty; the first winter we could not keep heating oil, and we were only trying to heat two rooms."

A friend from Kerwin Baptist Church in Kernersville, where the couple had been members while at the Winston-Salem Rescue Mission, came to visit. "Her eyes got as big as saucers" because she could not believe the living conditions of the parsonage. When she got back home and reported it to Pastor Joe Myers, he took up a special collection to buy carpeting for the young missionaries.

Someone had given Gail money for her birthday, which she happily invested in new linoleum for the kitchen.

Killing the roaches was a bit easier than getting rid of what was gnawing through her new cream and avocado green linoleum, which she selected to coordinate with that donated paint. One edge of the new linoleum stuck out under the porch door leading from the kitchen. Apparently a rat was living on the other side of that door on the old enclosed porch. Gail presumes it was the biggest wharf rat in town.

The tattered edge of that floor made her fearful what that rat could do to tiny Bethany. She set out a large tray of D-Con rat poison and, shockingly, the next morning the entire tray was eaten. She set a second tray out the next evening to be sure the rat was gone, but it disappeared too. For another two nights she had the same routine until apparently it was finally enough to kill the rodent.

Gail insists God prepared her for that house. The couple

moved to Durham on November 13, 1973. They intended to have the shelter operating within a few months. It took a year to get it going because of the economy, and in that time, Gail got used to the idea of giving up their cozy trailer to live full time at the Mission. They needed to be on hand to supervise the ministry 24 hours a day.

"I came to the point where I promised the Lord that if it meant living in a tent, I was willing to do that. I tell people that I didn't have to move in a tent, but that house was the next thing to it.

"I was prepared to live in the same house as the men, but God provided two separate houses, with the parsonage right behind the Mission," she said, characteristically counting her blessings.

"When we came here, we didn't know what we were getting into. Now I know those hardships."

Looking back, that blissful ignorance was probably for the best. If God had shown her how the ministry would grow and what her responsibilities as co-founder would become, she might have gone back home to mama in Winston-Salem, she laughs.

A fter a few years operating in the old two-story house, the Mission was crowded to capacity. It had room to house 12 men. However, there was never extra room to take in any more men in desperate need. The waiting list grew steadily, and Ernie's heart ached every time he had to turn someone away.

The Board of Directors (L–R: Wilburn Swaim, John King, Larry Carter, Ernie Mills, Rudolph Hardee) took a leap of faith when they voted to purchase the Fuller Memorial Presbyterian Church building.

For a couple of years, the "For Sale" sign had stood in front of Fuller Memorial Presbyterian Church. The graceful brick church built in 1929 with the four white pillars and beautiful arched stained glass windows was located at 1201 East Main Street, just one city block from the original Mission house. The church sits prominently at the corner of East Main Street and Alston Avenue, which is NC Highway 55, a main thoroughfare through northeast central Durham. Ernie would walk right past that church on his way to the old neighborhood A&P Grocery Store. It never occurred to him the building would be suitable for their purposes, primarily because he knew they would want far more money than the Mission could pay for it.

"My faith was so small," Ernie said. Eventually he got the message.

"We needed a much bigger facility. We finally did look at the church building, but they were asking $130,000 starting out. We didn't have that kind of money," Ernie said. Still, his conviction grew stronger that the Mission was supposed to be in that church and stay in that neighborhood.

"One day, I walked behind the church building and I saw a little crack in the brickwork. I reached in my pocket and pulled out a quarter. I walked up to that loose brick and stuck the quarter in the crack. As it fell down the interior wall, I knelt down and said, 'Lord, this is the first down payment on this building. I need you to send the rest if you want us to have this for your ministry."

Having found no other suitable or affordable locations, Ernie kept praying. He also kept making offers, trying to negotiate with the church elders.

"They would laugh at me. They were real friends of the Mission, but they needed enough to rebuild somewhere else. The crime rate was getting so high in the neighborhood that a lot of the older church members were just uncomfortable about coming downtown in this location," he explained.

Ernie persisted, offering $80,000. The church rejected the offer but came back two months later with a counteroffer. They would take $80,000 if they were allowed to remove the pews and stained glass windows from the chapel.

"I said, 'Man, if you take out the windows and the pews, I won't have a building.' Where would I get the money to replace them? It wasn't feasible for us," he said.

The church finally accepted $80,000 with no conditions.

There was just one problem: the Mission didn't have $80,000.

Ernie went to the bank, which would only loan $30,000

if the Mission could raise $10,000 for the down payment. Ernie decided to ask the church to hold the other half in a second mortgage. They agreed to carry the $40,000, and he had a deal.

There was just one more problem: the Mission didn't have the $10,000.

Ernie asked the church leader for one more thing he needed to seal that deal. Chuckling at his own audacity in asking for any more concessions, Ernie recalled the "something else" was a request to use the church sanctuary for a week to hold a Christmas Jubilee fundraiser. He needed that $10,000 he promised to the bank. He doesn't know why the church agreed to it, although a look back at the era of "stagflation," and the simultaneous decline of northeast central Durham might hold the clues.

East Durham boomed in the late 1800s and early 1900s. Homes and businesses were built to serve the workers at the Golden Belt Manufacturing cigarette wrapper plant as well as the nearby Durham Hosiery Mill, around which the northeast central Durham neighborhood grew.

In 1952, a large public housing development, intended to serve low income families, was built on the community gardens site located on the former Few Farm. The complex was named "Few Gardens" after the late Dr. W. P. Few, former president of Duke University. A lofty idea with noble intentions, it would be undermined by a changing social fabric.

By the mid-1970s, marijuana and cocaine deeply infiltrated the increasingly impoverished neighborhood. As drugs moved in, the neighborhood began its descent into urban blight. The increase in robberies and violent crime caused many long-time residents to flee to the suburbs, leaving poverty and disrepair in their wake.

Like so many public housing projects across the nation, the social environment deteriorated along with the crumbling buildings. Business and civic leaders began to disinvest in the area as drug dealers became entrenched.

Eventually, in 2003, bulldozers demolished Few Gardens as the beginning of a $35 million federally-funded revitalization plan for a 96-square block area east of downtown Durham, a blighted area which extended far beyond the public housing complex.

"Drugs really destroyed our neighborhood," said Ernie, recounting shocking and indelible images of the grip drugs took in the 1970s. Brazen dealers would set a bar stool in the middle of the street and service addicts in passing cars on either side. The area was a magnet for crack users and prostitutes.

Through the many years of the Mission's growth in the neighborhood, Ernie has had his share of frightening encounters. One day, as he was driving past a building the Mission had just purchased, he saw someone climbing in the back window. When he stopped the car to prevent the man from breaking into the building, a group of about 20 drug users and dealers surrounded him menacingly.

"Another man, a drug dealer, I think, came down the street and told them to leave me alone, saying, 'He's the preacher down at the Mission,'" and Ernie was unharmed. He later saw another man and then a woman come running out of the building and realized the man who was trying to reach the window wasn't trying to break in but was trying to peep at the prostitute.

The crime-ridden, poverty-stricken neighborhood, which still struggles with many of the same problems, has gone through dramatic periods of decline. One day a real estate developer named Bobby Roberts who had recently built a rental home nearby, got fed up and handed the house over to the Mission.

"He came into my office one day as mad as fire." He had just tried to show his well-kept property to prospective renters. When they saw a gang of crack dealers loitering nearby, they lost interest.

"He threw the keys on my desk and said, 'If you want it, you can have it. I'm not putting up with it any more.' Mr. Roberts went down to the courthouse and had the deed put in the Mission's name. It's the nicest and newest house we own," Ernie smiled.

"I've always felt safe here, even when it was a bad neighborhood. I know God wants me here. I'm not saying God has promised nothing bad will ever happen to me here, but I feel like I'm in God's will."

In 1978, when Fuller Memorial Presbyterian wanted to leave, Ernie was reassured he should stay in the neighborhood. The Jubilee at the church was a success. Through those nightly services, the $10,000 down payment was raised, despite the pressures of the Christmas season and the faltering economy.

Ernie uprooted the sign from the old location and carried it one block to the new location.

The church building became the new Durham Rescue Mission.

"I remember jiggling that big 4-foot-by-4-foot wooden Durham Rescue Mission sign out of the ground at the 1301 East Main Street house and putting it on my shoulders. Now, I'm no Samson, but I carried that sign one block down to the church and put it in front of the new Mission."

After that, he had to figure out how to manage that big church building, which was far beyond the scope of the Mission's existing budget. First of all, it meant moving his family from the six rooms they had at the Holman Street house into the cramped, 500-square-foot second-floor Sunday school classrooms he converted to living quarters at the church. He needed to be there to oversee the daily operations. They also had to prepare the original Mission house and parsonage for sale.

They divided a small upstairs Sunday school room by adding a wall. On one side, their "master bedroom" had just enough room for a double bed, literally. That meant they had to climb into it from the foot of the bed because there wasn't room to walk on either side. On the other side of the new partition was a tiny galley kitchen, and across the hall were two tiny closet-sized bedrooms for the children.

The Mission couldn't afford to heat and cool the chapel so Ernie closed it off, opening it only for four special services each year. He divided the basement fellowship hall into a combination chapel, dining room, and sitting area. Eventually, he was able to double the number of men served to 24, and when the budget increased, the church building would serve 40.

Ernie had negotiated an 8 percent loan with the bank and a similar rate for the church loan. When Fuller Memorial Presbyterian went to build their church building in the safer suburbs, they handed the second mortgage on the church over as payment to their builder, James Dunn.

Skyrocketing interest rates brought Dunn to see Ernie about getting his money. The second mortgage was given at 7 percent, and Dunn would have to pay 20 percent on borrowed construction money. Dunn told Ernie how badly he needed the mortgage paid off.

Ernie is elated, as he is assisted by board member Rev. Greg Allison to burn the mortgage on the 1201 E. Main St. church building property!

The Mission didn't have that kind of money, but when Dunn offered to cut 20 percent off the bottom line if he could have a cash payout, the frugal preacher had to take action. Durham's mayor at the time, Harry Rodenhizer, endorsed the Mission's plan by signing a letter to businesses and Mission supporters. It explained what a great deal it was to save 20 percent and years of interest. In actuality, each dollar they donated would be worth three.

"Donations started coming in. I was amazed at the response. We were able to completely raise all that money. Ask and you shall receive. That's really the history of the Mission since 1973," Ernie said.

Meanwhile, during the move to the church, Ernie found a buyer for the old house, parsonage, and tiny storefront where the Mission began. With banks still reluctant to loan money for real estate in the blighted neighborhood, the Mission held the mortgage themselves—another compassionate move no one realized at the time would prove beneficial to the Mission in years to come.

For a decade, the real estate investor who had several other rental properties, made his payments faithfully to the Mission.

In 1988, however, he found himself in financial trouble. He fell so far behind in his taxes that the city foreclosed and auctioned off the three buildings on the courthouse steps. As the mortgage holder, the Mission paid the delinquent taxes and got back all the property.

"We didn't need the property at the time, but we needed the income," said Gail.

As Ernie and Gail see it, God worked it out so the Mission could get income on the buildings but wouldn't get the buildings back until there was a need. After 10 years in the church, more space was needed for staff and residents. The first Mission house at 1301 East Main Street would become that much-needed staff quarters and office space when it became Mission property again in 1988. Ernie hadn't expected the Mission to ever outgrow the church. In fact, he had never expected it to outgrow that first house. But after another 10 years, in 1998, a still greater plan would unfold something Ernie had only dreamed about accomplishing. The Mission house where it all began became a shelter for single women.

After the daunting task of getting settled into the church building, Ernie could no longer ignore the growing number of requests for help from other communities.

Church leaders from Alamance County, in particular, nearly 45 minutes away, would often bring homeless men to the Durham Rescue Mission. They would tell him how much their own area needed a similar program. They gave financial support to the Durham Rescue Mission, but felt their communities would give more to a mission based in their own area. It was just a matter of getting it started.

Ernie began scouting out locations for a mission in Alamance County. He visited the hub community of Burlington and neighboring Graham, and witnessed for himself the growing number of street people populating the region. A mission was sorely needed there. Ernie set about raising money to purchase a house to start a mission and finding people to staff it. Freshly graduated from Bible college, Tim Shoemaker, whose father had operated a rescue mission in Greenville, South Carolina, was their first live-in staff person. The Alamance Rescue Mission located at 129 West Holt Street in Burlington opened its doors to the needy in 1981.

A second mission meant dividing Ernie's time between the two locations.

To free him up, Ernie hired Robert Jones in 1981 to be his associate director of operations at the Durham facility. Making room for Jones and his family to live at the Mission meant

Ernie and Gail had to give up their 500-square-foot apartment on the second floor of the church building. Ernie found a house he wanted to buy in neighboring Orange County, on the Burlington side of Durham. Banks were less than enthusiastic to loan mortgage money to a preacher who relied solely on the kindness of contributors for his livelihood.

"I'd never been homeless before," said Ernie ironically. He eventually was able to assume the existing mortgage on the Orange County home and took out a small second mortgage to pay the rest. Finally, with their financing in place, the couple moved into their very first house, and the Jones family moved into the church building to oversee the Durham Rescue Mission 24-hours a day.

Robert Jones was born and raised in Northeast Central Durham. He describes the experience as going from dodging balls as a youth to dodging bullets as a grown-up. It wasn't just the roughness of the neighborhood that would mar his childhood years, though.

His father, a chronic alcoholic, and his mother, who had to be hospitalized from the stress brought on by their unstable life, divorced when he was 10. Robert, his older brother and two older sisters were placed in the Pittsboro Christian Children's Home for more than a year.

"Placing us in the children's home really snapped my father out of it," said Jones. "He came to a place in Alamance County called the Damascus Home. He came to know Christ as his personal savior."

His mother recovered and the couple reunited, regaining custody of the children. That was 1966, when Jones was 11. It was a happy time for the family, but it wouldn't last very long. His father died of a heart attack at age 41 after only a couple of years being back with the family.

It wasn't until he was 23 that Jones would find his way

God has used Pat and Robert Jones to "rescue the perishing" since 1982.

back to the Lord after years of drifting—years when he drank and did drugs, just like the people he hung out with. Blessed with a wry sense of humor, Jones said he masked his misery by always being the life of the party and class clown. His quick wit and ready one-liners likely cost him several grade points in high school, he conceded. It also kept him from dealing with his pain.

In 1978, he got married. His wife, Pat, who was an unbeliever, nonetheless accepted an invitation from friends to attend a church service at Bible Baptist Church in Durham. Pat normally came to every city-league softball game Robert played in. The same week they attended church, she was plagued with a sinus headache that wouldn't recede, so she decided at the last minute to stay home from one of Robert's softball games.

She was home when Dr. Arnold Goodman, a board member of the Durham Rescue Mission, knocked on the door. As a deacon at Bible Baptist Church, he was out on church visitation. Goodman came to follow up on their church visit to his Sunday school class the previous week and to share some scripture.

Although still adrift, Robert Jones always felt drawn to go back to church and knew he needed a personal relationship

Dr. Arnold Goodman

with Jesus Christ. When he walked into the house after the softball game that night, as Goodman was witnessing to his wife, he recognized immediately that, "The Lord had gripped Pat's heart and converted her."

That night, May 4, 1979, they both accepted Christ as their savior.

Before that night, for a long time Jones knew he was going against what he was supposed to be doing, distracting himself from his true purpose. It all began to change that night, he said. After their new Sunday school teacher left, they gathered the small amount of drugs that were in the house and flushed them down the toilet.

"We immediately began to surround ourselves with Christians," he said.

Within a matter of months they were praying for the Lord to show them what they were meant to do in His service. "I thought I was supposed to be a game warden. Then the Lord led me to the ministry, and I figured he had the wrong guy," he laughed.

He had already switched from working on a construction crew to working for the state in order to remove some destructive influences from his life. Then, in 1981, Ernie spoke to his church about some needs at the Mission, which included having some closets built.

Jones realized he had a week of vacation coming up, but his wife had to work, so he offered to build those closets. He remembers vividly watching Ernie juggle the pressing needs of the Mission. At one point, no fewer than eight people surrounded the pastor, saying, "Preacher, Preacher," clamoring for his attention for different and equally important reasons.

"Boy, I'm glad it's him and not me," is the thought Jones recalled having at the time. "Little did I know Ernie would

Robert, Pat, and Tracey Jones

have such an impact on us."

Less than a year after that indelible impression was made, Jones was in charge of daily operations at the Durham Rescue Mission. His wife joined him shortly afterwards, working in the office, and their first child, Tracey, was born in February, 1982.

Jones would also often accompany Ernie on his trips to Burlington during the days when the new Mission was getting started. He was very involved in the planning, and he was the one who suggested the name "Alamance Rescue Mission," so as not to leave out towns that surround the Burlington area where it was to be located.

But life took another detour; one he realizes now was the perfect training ground for what God wanted him to do. Even though Jones was not an ordained minister, the Rev. Greg Allison asked Jones to become the associate pastor at Bible Baptist Church. It was a tough decision, made all the more difficult by Ernie's obvious disappointment.

Still, Jones felt led to take the new opportunity rather than stay in mission work at that time.

"I wasn't ready. I was learning what I needed to learn. I went on staff at the church, and those five years were more valuable to me than any college courses," Jones said.

Having observed Jones working at the Mission and then the church, Ernie knew he would be the ideal person to lead the Alamance Rescue Mission. Five years after Jones left his employ at the Durham Rescue Mission, Ernie approached him about becoming the director of the Alamance Rescue

Mission.

Ernie knew from the beginning that Jones was supposed to be in Burlington, and says the phenomenal growth of the ministry under Jones' leadership is a testimony to how God has blessed his obedience in accepting that position.

In 2004, the Alamance Rescue Mission moved from its original two-story quarters into a 25,500-square-foot former school building, with five acres of land located at 1519 North Mebane Street. The Mission has expanded from serving only men to include a crisis pregnancy center and is a growing ministry.

Chapter 12
SHATTERED LEG, SHATTERED LIFE RESTORED

Most people come to the Mission as a respite from the swirling chaos of their lives. They are invited to stay as long as they are seeking help for their problems.

In 1982, Billy Bullock thought it was perfectly reasonable to be living in the woods off of Interstate 85 in Durham. Long at odds with his family and a bit of rebel in school, the defiant youth had rejected authority at all levels of his life.

Addicted, unemployed, homeless, and aimless, Bullock didn't realize how hopeless he had become at such a young age. He was just unlucky, he thought. One night that year, the long-haired 22-year-old vagrant walked across the Interstate, intending to meet up with some friends to party. Silently, he hoped the state trooper who had stopped a motorist nearby would not cite him for jay walking.

He didn't see the car that hit him because he was looking at the blue flashing lights. As he looks back, Bullock realizes that if that trooper hadn't been there, the ambulance wouldn't have raced to the scene as quickly as it did, with paramedics treating his multiple severe injuries within minutes.

Bullock wound up at the Mission with a leg that was literally shattered by the accident. Although it didn't occur to him at the time, he now knows it was really his shattered life that brought him there. Drugs, alcohol, and no sense of direction were major problems that needed addressing, as were the emotional issues that led to those choices. The accident was the vehicle that allowed that work to begin. The broken leg prevented him from running away and avoiding his past.

"The only thing holding that leg together was my skin," he said. His lower leg was broken in several places. In addition, his femur in that same leg was snapped in two, making recovery a long process. He had to have pins put in his lower leg and a rod placed in his hip.

Along with multiple lacerations, his left shoulder bone was chipped; a vertebra in his neck was fractured; his spleen and liver were both bruised.

He spent two months recuperating in the hospital while neither friends nor family came to visit. The hospital was getting ready to release him. His family had given up on him, and he had nowhere to go.

"If I didn't have this place to come to, I wouldn't have been saved," Bullock said. "I'd be dead. I probably would have died of my sins—if not drugs, then in some other way."

Always skeptical of authority, Bullock refers to his former self as a "hard sell." While he had the aptitude for the class work in high school, he couldn't handle the rules and regulations. He'd been kicked out of ROTC. College was out of the question, he'd decided, because of finances. That's when he started partying, visiting his friends that did go to local colleges, but only for entertainment and to get high.

At the Mission, he had to follow the rules. In a full leg-cast and with no other options, for

Billy Bullock (left on the 2nd row) came to the mission in 1982.

once he decided to keep his nose clean. For a lot of people, he said, it's a last hope. As long as they have insurance, hospitals or other programs will take them. In his case, not having that option and having to go along with what he considered a "last hope," turned out to be the life-altering hope he needed.

"The changes were slow. I did get off the drugs, and then later I quit smoking in 1985."

For the first time in his life, Bullock said he began to listen. Sometimes, to his amazement, his questions about faith were answered. He became a Christian and eventually began attending Cedar Grove Bible Institute, in Cedar Grove, North Carolina.

"Every verse and every book is so interrelated. It's amazing how perfect the Bible really is and how little the average person knows about it," Bullock said.

He considers attending Bible college a privilege, a dramatic change in his academic life. Another change has been within his family, which rejected him as a rebellious youth. He worked hard to restore his relationship with the family, and now he has taken on a leadership role in caring for his aging father.

Bullock received Supplementary Social Security disability for 10 years after the accident. In 1992, Bullock gave up his disability check when Ernie asked him to become the purchasing agent for the Mission, where he still works today.

Billy Bullock is now the purchasing agent for the Durham Rescue Mission.

Bethany Mills never sat down to a traditional Thanksgiving family dinner until she got married. Even now, Bethany (whose married name is Stroup) alternates celebrating Thanksgiving between her husband's family and the Durham Rescue Mission, where her

Bethany and Robert Stroup are the pianist and director of mission choirs. Robert adds to the musical presentation by playing his trumpet!

parents have invariably spent every Thanksgiving since she was born in 1974.

"Every family has their traditions," laughed Bethany, who lived at the Mission from the time she was born until she was 8 and the family moved to neighboring Orange County in 1982. Even then, if she wasn't in school, she was usually at the Mission, whether it was weekends or holidays.

As a baby and toddler, she lived in the parsonage at 106 North Holman Street, directly behind the original Mission house. Later, she lived in the upstairs apartment of the church building and slept in a bedroom about the size of a closet, with barely enough room for a twin bed and one small chest of drawers.

Today, her husband Robert directs the men's and women's Victory choirs, with Bethany playing the piano. To her,

"Ambassador Caleb" with Joy Smith

the Mission residents remain her extended family. With all of her fond memories of growing up at the Mission, she never hesitates to bring her son Caleb, who was born in 2001, along for their weekly choir practice. The residents dote on the boy as much as they did on Bethany and her brother Ernie Jr. when they were children.

Caleb proudly wears his "Durham Rescue Mission Ambassador" lapel pin as he hands out brochures when the choirs are invited to churches to sing and share testimony about how their lives have changed since coming to the Mission.

Many of the residents grew special to Bethany. As a tot, Bethany had a penchant for taking off one shoe. Gail would often look out the parsonage window to see old K.B. Lynch

"Grandpa George Bunn." Many times when Ernie had to be out of town, Mr. Bunn would be in charge of the mission.

patiently helping the little girl put her shoe back on.

And then there was "Grandpa George" Bunn, who had come to the Mission at an advanced age. An alcoholic, Bunn was disabled and unable to work anymore. Throughout his life, he had worked odd jobs and never paid Social Security taxes, so he couldn't live on the small government check he received.

The benevolent old-timer lived at the Mission until his

death. He became a surrogate grandfather to the little girl who never knew her real grandfathers. Bunn still holds a special place in her heart.

Once sober, he became a trusted resident supervisor, a crusty character with an unforgettable cackle. He was a dependable soul upon whom everyone there relied. He died of cancer when Bethany was away at nursing school at Bob Jones University.

"The residents had to earn my parent's trust," she said, remembering the strict guidelines her Dad and Mom had devised to keep the children safe. Once the residents proved themselves trustworthy, many of them became like family members, and treated Bethany and her brother, Ernie, Jr., as favorite grandchildren. Those same residents looked to Ernie and Gail for guidance just as much as Bethany did. But she got used to sharing her parents a long time ago. She didn't feel they divided their attention so much as they multiplied it.

"They never missed a basketball game when I was playing," she said.

Watching the way her parents interacted with the homeless people at the Mission gave her a unique perspective on humanity. Many of them had been rejected by their own families, yet her parents welcomed them with open arms. It was a lesson learned by observation more than instruction and has no doubt brought

Bethany during her "Pinning Ceremony" at Bob Jones University, where she graduated with a bachelor of science degree in nursing. Bethany is now a registered nurse at Duke University Medical Center—the same hospital where she was a premature baby in 1974!

compassion into her nursing career at Duke University Hospital.

Likewise, her older brother Ernie, Jr. knew at an early age that he had a life that was quite different than other kids they knew. One thing he remembers vividly is they did not have a television in their house. He would occasionally sneak a peek at friends' houses just to see the programs they were always talking about. He knows he played more outdoors and used his imagination more than his friends.

Their lives were also different because he and Bethany attended a Christian school. They also traveled a lot more than their friends because his dad would be invited to preach at churches throughout the Southeast.

"When you think about travel, you think about having a lot of money. But it was exactly the opposite. Dad was going to different churches for speaking engagements to raise money," said Ernie Jr. (although he dropped the "junior" long ago).

Even the family trip to Disney World was a mix of Mission business and pleasure. Ernie was invited to speak at a church in Orlando.

"We did get to go, but the flip side of that coin was that Daddy drove straight through," so they wouldn't have to pay for a hotel, he said. Twelve hours was a long trip for little kids in the back of a Chevrolet Chevette with no air conditioning.

Ernie with the family for a relaxing time by the campfire—another "thrifty vacation"!

Ernie Junior's colorful memories of life at the Mission aren't run of the mill childhood recollections. Some were bad in his opinion—like having to sing in front of the congregations when his dad was visiting churches for support. He hated that. But some were fascinating, like that time his dad found the gas space heater on top of the trash heap just when he'd given up hope of heating the new Mission house. The dump was not just a dropping off experience. He always found something interesting to spark his vivid imagination.

"I always took something back with me from the dump, and the funny thing is Daddy did, too," he said of his thrifty, waste-not, want-not upbringing.

It was all a bit different than the average childhood, but the main difference was the way he witnessed lives changed by the Gospel. Those transformations left lasting impressions.

His memories of Grandpa George are more of the mischief variety, like when the kids would grab his cigarettes and run as fast as they could because they knew they were bad for him.

"Mom would try to keep us away from the new guys at first. There have been murderers, rapists, robbers; guys that have committed any vice, every crime imaginable. That's what a rescue mission is," said Ernie Jr., who went on to study criminal justice at his father's alma mater, Bob Jones University and became a Durham County Sheriff's deputy.

Ernie Jr. said his father would make it a point to take him hunting and fishing so they could be alone. It was a

Ernie, Jr., carries on the family calling of "protecting and serving."

Father and son enjoy their labor of a long night of "flounder gigging."

rare chance for the son to glimpse "Dad" instead of "Preacher Mills." Even so, it didn't matter what city dignitary was in his dad's office; the boy was never turned away. He could come skipping unannounced into the office bouncing a basketball and have his father's undivided attention. Just like for Bethany, at least one of his parents made it to every basketball game he played in school. And while Preacher Ernie Mills had never heard "I love you" from his own father, he never let a day go by without telling his son how much he loved him.

Ernie Jr. remembers Mission residents putting themselves in harm's way to protect him. Once, a vagrant with a knife accosted him because he was throwing rocks at pigeons. From out of nowhere, one of the men stopped the attack and sent the vagrant on his way.

"I believe most of the Mission residents would be willing to sacrifice their lives for my mom or my dad. They were very protective of me," he said. "I think that whole dynamic of having me and my sister there, and thinking they should be an example, helped some of them change."

Wade Hursey was one of those guys. A former minor league baseball player, he was the finest mechanic in Durham, Ernie Jr. said.

"There was nothing on wheels Wade couldn't fix or soup up. But Wade couldn't lay the bottle down. He couldn't keep a job."

The Mission nursed him back to health when he arrived.

The friendly, warm hearted man never taught the young lad how to play ball, but he taught him a lot about fixing cars. Since Ernie Jr. was more of a car fanatic than a sports fan—that was just fine with him.

Hursey came and left the Mission three different times. Each time he would leave, he would start drinking again, and the Mission would sober him up when he returned months later. The final time he was sobered up and back as part of the Mission family, he started receiving a disability check from Social Security. With his newfound income, he was soon gone again, never to return. Soon afterwards, Ernie Jr. saw Hursey for the last time, unconscious in a hospital bed, just before he died from cirrhosis of the liver. Ernie Jr. was 18, and to him it was a painful illustration of how money is not the answer to an addiction.

Another indelible memory of a Mission resident was a former Durham city police officer who was hooked on cocaine. When he arrived strung out at the Mission, Ernie Jr. was confused because he was always told that police were there to help you, and this one needed help himself.

On the one hand, he answered the young boy's persistent questions and wrote down what all the 10-codes on the police radio meant. Ernie Jr. memorized them all.

"He taught me how to spin a car around," Ernie Jr. said.

On the other hand, he was a living example of what not to do.

His Sunday school teacher, Russell May, at Bible Baptist Church, was also a police officer and became a strong influence on his future career in law enforcement. He never wanted to be a fireman like most of his friends. He wanted to protect and serve, like May. He wanted to help people like he watched his dad do at the Mission all his life.

ERNIE'S SOCIAL EXPERIMENT

Experiencing homelessness for himself.

hen Ernie Jr. was 17, his father asked him to go "undercover" with him to find out what it really meant to be homeless. It was an idea that held strong appeal to the future deputy, but scared the daylights out of his mother.

For all of his 20-plus years of helping the homeless and his great empathy for their plight, in 1989 Ernie realized he still didn't truly know what it was like to walk in their tattered shoes.

Occasionally, a resident would grumble at his work assignment, and Ernie would remind him that it was a working mission. Invariably, the man would counter that Ernie didn't know what it was like to face the hardships he had gone through. Ernie had to admit that was true.

So, in typical Ernie Mills, learn-by-doing fashion, the resolute preacher decided he needed to see the world from a homeless person's perspective.

"The Lord just laid on my heart that I should see what it's like to live on the streets. I had never been homeless, and I couldn't completely understand what it was like. I'd never had to beg for my food. I'd never had to beg for my clothes. I always had a place to sleep," Ernie said.

He started growing out his hair and beard and told the staff who were used to him wearing a tie every day why he might be looking a little unkempt in weeks to come. His smooth, wavy mane became an unruly bristly mass, not growing long so much as out, like an afro. Scruffy whiskers covered most of his normally clean-shaven jaw line. With some worn out jeans and a threadbare shirt, he was ready for his social experiment of being homeless.

His plan was to find the most threatening streets in America and head there anonymously to see how difficult it would be for a homeless person to find food, shelter, work, and friendship.

August 1989. Ernie let his hair and beard grow as he prepared to live on the streets of Washington, DC, as a "homeless person" with 17-year-old Ernie, Jr.

He settled on Washington, D. C.

When Gail heard what he planned to do, and that he planned to take her only son with him, she stoically silenced her fears, trusting God would protect them.

"All I knew was that it was Murder Capital USA!" she exclaimed, reminiscing and showing staff members the pictures of the unrecognizable pair, looking scruffy in their shabby attire.

Ernie decided a week would give him the exposure he felt he needed to fully understand the perspective of those he was trying to help. But even then, he knew he could always call Gail at any time and say, "Honey, come get me." Homeless people have usually exhausted all those options.

"I had never been homeless myself. Yes, I had a dad that was an alcoholic, but he always maintained a home, and we never went hungry," he said.

It was not that fending for himself on the most dangerous streets in America was an appealing idea. "The idea came from the Lord, because I know I didn't want to go."

Ernie Jr. took a day to mull it over and then decided he

wasn't going to let his dad venture into that situation by himself. Looking back, he's quite certain that at 17 he didn't fully understand the danger "two middle class, naïve white guys" would face walking the crime-ridden, predominantly black inner city streets of Washington, D. C.

Ernie Sr.'s one concern was what he was going to say when people asked him why he was homeless. "I knew I wouldn't lie."

The Lord took that burden away, he said, just as the intrepid duo rolled into Manassas, Virginia right outside D. C. The alternator went bad on the aging Ford Fairmont station wagon and the car conked out. Now they had a true story about having to raise enough money to fix the car so they could get home. They parked the broken-down car at the house of their friend, Jack Booth. His sister, Donna Mickle, on staff at the Mission, had arranged for Booth to keep the preacher's car for the week.

They divested themselves of their wallets and watches, leaving all their identification and valuables with Booth. Ernie Sr. even took off his wedding ring for fear of becoming a mugging target. They would go without money, provisions or even a comb in their pockets.

Booth dropped them off at the nearest Metro stop leading into D. C., and they immediately had to start panhandling for change to pay for their subway ride. One couple actually gave the pair all their change and the four rode companionably together on the trip downtown. When they reached the National Mall, they began immediately talking to homeless people, asking where they could find a place to sleep for the night.

Their first stop would be the Gospel Rescue Mission, and they were directed down a foul-smelling dumpster-lined alley behind a Chinese restaurant. They stood in line near the rotting garbage and were told they needed $2 up front to stay the night. Feeling confident they would get in because they were near the front of the line, they soon learned that those who stayed the previous night had priority over newcomers like them.

The line was divided in two, and they were not in the line of the ones who stayed the night before. The mission filled up before they could get in. By the time they were turned away that afternoon, an uncharacteristically chilly August rain began to fall. Nerves frayed from the uncertainty and shivering with no jackets, their rumbling stomachs reminded them they had not eaten since breakfast. They had come early though, so they were hopeful they would find a safe place to sleep that night.

They saw a group of Boy Scouts as they set out to find another place to stay and asked them for money to eat, but no one would oblige. At about 4 p.m., they talked a begrudging hot dog vendor to give them each a hot dog on a bun. Not full by any means, they asked a fruit and vegetable vendor for some produce, which he disgustedly refused to give. At the Salvation Army, they picked up a list of places to get a free meal in the city.

They learned where the soup kitchens were, and that mobile food wagons made specific stops at various street corners throughout the day. One would be stopping on the corner of 14th Street and Maryland Avenue at 7 p.m. So, with only a few minutes to get there, they started hustling to be there on time.

On the way, they met up with another man whom they had seen turned away at the Gospel Rescue Mission earlier. Their diversion made them miss the 7 o'clock food wagon. Another one was scheduled for 9:30 at 18th Street and Pennsylvania Avenue, so they struck out with Archie, their newfound D. C. friend. They were on time this time, gratefully devouring the sandwich, orange, and hot tea from the wagon.

It was approaching 10 p.m., their first rainy night in a strange city, and they still had no place to stay. Archie said he knew about a shelter, so they decided to try that one. When they arrived, they learned it was only for women. The woman who answered the door, however, told them to stay put outside and she'd make a call for them. In the meantime, a patrolman came and told them to move along. They were allowed to stay when the woman at the mission said a van would be picking them up to take them to an emergency shelter. They waited in the drizzle for about an hour in their shirt sleeves, but a van did arrive to take them to a place called the Blair Night Shelter.

Before entering their new refuge, they saw about 50 "rough, rugged, cursing, fussing men" arguing outside. Inside, they were gruffly asked for their social security numbers and shown to a dingy room with pealing paint, lined with rows of single beds on wheels.

Ernie Jr. said that night left one of the strongest memories of that homeless week with his father. Whenever men arrive at the Durham Rescue Mission, they get a clean, safe place to sleep, and both Ernies had similar expectations for their stay in D. C. They were in for a rude awakening.

"Daddy said, 'I really appreciate you taking us in. If you just give me the sheets, I'll make the beds up.'"

The shelter attendant just laughed harshly and told them they should be happy to have a place to sleep and walked away.

"The beds had old plastic mattresses with cracks all in them where the cotton was sticking out. You could smell the nastiest mix of urine, puke and booze. Daddy normally sleeps on his back, but I'm a stomach sleeper. He pulled off his undershirt for me to use as a pillow. We were out of the rain, but we had to sleep with our shoes on because they would steal your shoes," Ernie Jr. said.

He slept some that night, but his father didn't close his eyes, listening to the vulgar language and staying alert for any dangers from the hostile stares directed at them from the sea of unfamiliar and unfriendly faces. The preacher was up by 4:30 a.m., asking around if anyone knew where he could find work. He learned a van picked men up for day labor jobs at 5:30, so he roused Ernie Jr., put his t-shirt back on, and headed for the van. A crush of men loaded onto the van, separating the father and son. The elder wound up in the back and the son was crammed in between seats at the front.

"The guy next to me was yelling, 'Get off me. I don't need no filthy cracker all over me. Somebody busted him in the back of the head,'" recalled the younger half of the duo, so the crowded van made it to the construction job site without further incident.

They had to stand in line to rent steel-toed boots, which were ripped and had no laces. They bought two sandwiches for breakfast and went right to work by 7:30, sweeping up construction debris and carrying it down the numerous flights of stairs. Quitting time was 3:30 p.m., but the van didn't come to pick them up until 5. The homeless crew received checks at the end of the day for their hard work, and the van driver obligingly stopped at a liquor store where they could cash their checks. Most bought beer or wine, including the driver, who soon pulled off the road to eat a sandwich and drink his wine.

Ernie Jr. cashed his check because he had to have a Mountain Dew and some salt and vinegar potato chips. Ernie Sr. made a big show of writing "For Deposit Only" on the back of his check, in hopes of not getting robbed. He said that his wife could use the money a whole lot more than he could, and he was going to mail it home to her.

That night, they were advised by other more experienced D. C. street people that the Pearce School Shelter was a better place to stay. Because the van driver had taken his time getting back to the Blair Street Shelter, they were too late for supper when they finally got to Pearce. All that was offered to eat was sauerkraut and potatoes. The shower, although just a cavernous open pit with a garden hose, at least gave them a chance to rinse off the construction dust. Then, when Ernie Jr. returned to his bed, the pants he had left lying there were still on top, but the pockets were emptied of the remains of his paycheck. Before they turned in that second night, another D. C. friend named Charles came to visit, and they had a nice conversation.

It would not be the restful refuge they were seeking. A fight soon broke out, with drunken men brawling and kicking each other, making it an even more fearful night than their first. Loud snoring was interrupted only by the noise of one occupant kicking the offender awake. The next morning was Saturday, and after a good breakfast, they went with two friends, who were already drunk, to a church that gave out clothing the second Saturday of the month. They met the preacher, who apologized, but said the church wasn't giving away clothing that day.

They headed back to the shelter for lunch with their drunken friend Charles, who immediately began badmouthing the staff. He became so unruly, he was asked to leave.

They were determined to find some clean clothes to change after their two grungy days and nights in the city.

It was bad enough that Ernie Sr. had only a plastic fork to comb his bristly afro. He couldn't stand to stay in those clothes another day. The pair was directed to a mission, but when they saw the crowd outside playing loud soul music, they knew it was a different clientele than the shelters they had been at. It wasn't winos or alcoholics. It was crack addicts and prostitutes.

Still, the shelter staff was helpful and gave them all the clothing they needed. They headed to the National Mall for a nap. Then Ernie Jr. charmed a grandmotherly type and a businessman for enough money to get them over to the Gospel Rescue Mission. About to be turned away again, a staff member waved them back as they began walking away. They went to the chapel for services and afterwards were pleasantly surprised that the beds they would be sleeping in that night had clean sheets.

Having accomplished the task of finding work within 12 hours of arriving, Ernie Sr. wanted to learn more about life on the streets. They spent their days panhandling and talking to street people, experiencing for themselves the indignity of not having a home. They found a church that agreed to call a junk yard and pay for a rebuilt alternator to fix his car. When he got back to Durham, of course, he mailed a check to the church to cover the expense and thanked them for their charity.

The story might have become Mission folklore, nothing more than a local legend within the mission walls, if it hadn't been captured on film by a local television station. But, say Ernie and Gail, God must have wanted the general public to hear about it and perhaps think more about what it would be like to really have nowhere to turn.

The day before Ernie was to leave Durham for D. C., a reporter called from the local CBS television affiliate, WRAL, wanting to speak with him. The reporter was doing a story about homelessness and wanted to interview Ernie the next day. Gail took the call and explained why her husband wouldn't be around for a week. The reporter got more than he bargained for.

"He said, 'We want to come over there and get shots of him packing to go,'" Gail quoted the reporter.

"Packing? He's not taking anything!" Gail replied.

Ernie declined any interviews before he left, fearing it would blow his cover. Instead, he arranged for the television crew to meet him in D. C. at the end of his week-long adventure. He and Ernie Jr. agreed to wear wireless microphones, as the crew followed at a distance so as not to be detected, and thus get an accurate picture of life on the streets. The television station turned the story into a two-night series on the evening news.

Ernie learned many things from his trip that changed his ministry to meet the physical and emotional needs of the people the Durham Rescue Mission serves.

"Feeling how a homeless person is treated on the streets made me more determined that our staff would know the importance of showing respect to every person who comes to the Mission," Ernie said.

Chapter 15
THE VICTORY PROGRAM
Trusting God to overcome addiction.

While the 1980s was a decade of expansion for the Mission, the 1990s were a time of reflection, re-evaluation, and dramatic change. For the first time, the Mission opened a shelter for women and children. Its approach to addiction recovery then underwent a complete overhaul.

"In the beginning, I was under the impression that if a guy was homeless, his problem was that he needed a job and money. They would come to the mission and be on a one-week restriction while we dried them out. Then we would go out and help them get a job," Ernie said.

What habitually happened next was that by the first or second paycheck, they would go out and get high. Soon Ernie realized that a cocaine addict doesn't need money.

"Really, that could be the worst thing for him. Literally, we were enabling them. We were giving them a place to stay until they could earn some money to get their next fix. That was hurting them. Until they have control of themselves, they can't control the money."

The Mission developed a more intense program for the addicted men, comprised of Bible study, vocational training, and counseling, calling it the Victory Program. The name is from I Corinthians 15:57: "But thanks *be* to God, which giveth us the victory through our Lord Jesus Christ."

The Victory Program changed the mission's previous policy of letting the men go out to work after one week of sobriety to six months of rehabilitation before they were allowed to find a job. It allowed them to spend the time beginning the process of gaining victory over their addiction.

The longer wait turned out to be a weaning process and another step of faith for the Mission, which was dependent upon the $7 a day their employed residents were required to pay for their keep. The Mission counted on that income as a big percentage of its operating budget.

"It was a testing of my faith in that area," Ernie said. There were fears that the men wouldn't stay if they couldn't earn money.

Ernie agonized over the decision. Finally, after a lot of prayer, he decided he was willing to risk going so far as to close the Mission if the program wasn't effective.

"We were not seeing enough changed lives. We did lose a few men because of that restriction. But we had to change what we were doing. It wasn't working," Ernie said.

Income was down for the first few months, he said, "But God began to raise up extra donations, and it gave us a much better program where the men could focus on their drug problem and let the Lord help them solve that drug problem."

In the Victory Program, members start the day with breakfast at 6 a.m. and Bible study at 6:30, followed by personal chore time from 7 until 8, when they receive their work assignments for the day. The men attend four hours of classes from 8 a.m. to noon, eat lunch, and then begin their job assignments around the Mission. Just as Ernie did from the beginning, the staff makes it a point to find out what skills each person has—talents they might not even know they possess—to help determine their job assignments.

After six months, the men transition into temporary job assignments in the community, instead of just working on campus at the Mission. Ernie established "Temps to the Rescue," a non-profit temporary employment agency to make employers more comfortable with hiring recovering addicts or rehabilitated convicted felons.

Since Ernie had seen the reluctance of companies to give the residents a chance, he came up with the idea of the Mission serving as the intermediary. This way, the employer wouldn't have the difficulties of firing someone if it didn't work out. Another incentive to hire Mission residents was that Temps to the Rescue would be paying all of the taxes and insurances. It grew into a way to transition the former addicts into productive members of society.

The residents continue to attend their morning Bible studies and to receive individual biblical counseling for their problems and addictions.

The teaching of the Bible is what alters their thinking, said the Rev. Rob Tart, chief operating officer of the Mission. He explained that the Mission counsels from a biblical standpoint, allowing the Word of God to effect the changes in their hearts and lives.

Clearly, from the Mission's perspective, what everyone needs most is to receive the Gospel, no matter what their circumstances. They also need structure, security, discipline, and rules, just like everyone else in society.

"I think a lot of people have a tentativeness around homeless people. They are not sure how to react to them. We view them as no different (from anyone) be-

Robert Tart, Chief Operating Officer, oversees the large mission family as well as caring for his four children— Katie, Brittany, Heidi, and Alex—and his lovely wife, Lydia.

cause they aren't," said Tart.

"Here, they have to get up early in the morning and work. It's amazing how quickly they bounce back and they look 'normal' again," Tart said. "They are given work, and they hear Bible teachings regularly. This keeps down the violence and keeps attitudes in check. We don't have near the trouble that other facilities have, where they feel they have to somehow enforce with force, and you hear a lot of angry yelling. The difference here is the regular preaching of the Word of God."

After a decade of ministering to the homeless at the Mission, Tart is still amazed at how quickly a person's appearance improves once they are offered a respite and some responsibility. It is an outward sign of what is going on inside them, said Tart.

His ability to connect with the residents and to translate Ernie's ideas into actions has made Tart an invaluable addition to the Mission, Ernie and Gail said.

He came to work at the Mission in 1995 straight out of graduate school at Bob Jones University. After high school, however, Tart didn't have any specific plans for going to college.

He was working as an assistant manager at a McDonald's, and then Burger King hired him away for the same position, and then promoted him to manager. They sent him to Aschaffenburg, Germany to manage a store. He had been a Christian since childhood, but in Germany, he got serious about it, and began attending a church where an American missionary served as pastor.

He quit his fast food job in 1989 to attend Bob Jones, where he earned a Bachelor of Arts degree in Christian Missions and a master's in teaching Bible.

After he graduated at age 30, he called the Mission because he had known of it growing up in Fayetteville, North Carolina. Ernie invited him to come for a visit, and hired him as Mission chaplain.

What drew him to the Mission was it's adherence to the Bible, and what drew Ernie to Tart was his love for the Bible and his education. Ernie soon saw how invaluable his managerial and problem solving skills were at the Mission.

Rob has a masters degree in teaching Bible, and this has equipped him to counsel the hurting men who are seeking help at the mission.

Tart oversees the daily operation of the Mission, and organizes special community outreach events that happen periodically throughout the year. He preaches most Sunday mornings at the Mission chapel. He supervises the Victory program, leads morning devotions, and teaches morning classes Monday through Friday.

"He is Ernie's right hand man, and has taken a great deal of the daily burden of running the Mission off Ernie's shoulders," said a grateful Gail Mills.

Tart said looking back, it's probably not a job he would have envisioned doing at a young age.

"But in all honesty, I do the same thing I've done since I was 18, and that's manage people," he said of his fast food managerial experience. "In many ways, it's the same people."

Since the early days of the Mission, Ernie would often share with board members how much he wanted to be able to also help women. He was especially burdened by the needs of homeless mothers with children. In the late 1980s, evidence of a changing society was visible in the growing numbers of women out on the streets, along with their even more vulnerable children.

There just never seemed to be a way to provide the services within the confines of the Mission's limited space. They never expected to outgrow the two-story house where they started, and certainly didn't anticipate the church building would fill up so quickly. There was just no feasible way to mix the male and female populations. They would give food and clothing to the women who came for help, and try to find them places to stay.

Even after Ernie and Gail found someone to supervise overnight at the church building and they moved out, they were known to occasionally take a woman in need into their own home if she had nowhere else to go.

Their kindness was long remembered by May Jordan, who was one of those women in 1984, who wrote to the couple years later to tell them how much their help meant in her life:

> Dear Rev. Mills,
>
> Thank you for giving me the opportunity to help others as you helped me and my two younger chil-

*dren 19 years ago just after Thanksgiving. You
didn't just give us a roof for the night, it was with
you and your wife since at that time there was
only men staying at the Mission at night. I'll
never forget your kindness and I'll always help
someone else where I can.*

May R. Jordan

Back in those days, even though Ernie was always one
to see opportunities where others see obstacles, he could
not envision how his desire to help homeless women, children, and even families would work itself out.

It started slowly, in March of 1990, when the Mission
purchased a two-story home at 1209 East Main Street for
$25,000. The house was to serve as the new shelter for wom-
en and preschool children, and was located just a few houses
down from the church. As the fall approached, excitement
grew about embarking on this new ministry as the extensive and time-consuming renovation neared completion.

Then, on a cold October night, a transient broke in to get
warm. He built a fire in the fireplace and left it unattended.
Months of work and years of dreams went up in flames as
the blaze destroyed the newly remodeled home.

Ernie shook his head at the irony of that event. If the
homeless man had simply knocked at the church door just
down the street, he not only could have had a comfortable
warm bed but nice hot meals and some encouraging company as well.

Devastated staff members asked the beleaguered
preacher why God would allow such a tragedy to happen.
Certainly just as disappointed and bewildered, Ernie didn't
know why it had happened. However, as always, he knew

God was in control. He assured everyone that God would get glory out of the catastrophe.

Meanwhile, the Mission had other needs, and he didn't have time to let them go unattended. One of the Mission's greatest expenses was providing heat and hot water to its growing campus of houses surrounding the church.

Always on the lookout for money-saving ideas, Ernie was captivated by an exhibition at the North Carolina State Fair in Raleigh that fall. Tim Phillips, who sold Taylor Water Stoves based in Virginia, was demonstrating his equipment at the fair.

The wood burning stove—originally designed at North Carolina State University—could heat several houses and supply all the heat and hot water the Mission needed. That stove would mean a huge savings, and Ernie was determined to buy one if he could. Ernie couldn't resist sharing his enthusiasm about the product with the vendor. Then, out of habit, he began sharing with Phillips about the work of the Mission. Phillips said he just had to come and check it out for himself.

Phillips ended up donating the Taylor Water Stove and enlisted several of his vendors to donate their time and necessary pipes and parts for the installation. The value of all that equipment totaled $25,000—the same amount the Mission had paid for the house that burned down. Everyone felt God had restored the money that was lost to the fire and provided for a long-term solution to the Mission's heating and hot water expenses.

When Ernie began looking for sources of wood, he learned the city had to pay dumping fees at its own landfill when it had to remove trees from city property.

Ernie happily invited the city to bring its discarded wood to the Mission to feed "Old Bertha," the nickname the Mission gave their Taylor Water Stove. That saved the city dumping fees and saved the Mission money on buying wood. Ernie liked the idea of recycling the wood that otherwise would take up space rotting at the landfill, and of reducing the Mission's dependence upon oil.

A still greater plan began to unfold a few months later in 1991 when the Mission received an unexpected $35,000 bequest from the estate of Nannie V. Webster.

Unbeknownst to Ernie and Gail, Webster, a Durham resident, had once toured the Mission with her Sunday school class, which collected paper towels and toilet paper to donate.

As far as anyone could deduce, she had only visited the Mission once and had then instructed her attorney to include the Mission in her will.

The Mission staff was overwhelmed with Mrs. Webster's humble and generous gift. The Mission had never received such a large single donation. When the check was presented to Ernie—after he got up off the floor where he'd fainted, as he likes to joke—his first thoughts were, "Lord, what are your plans for this money?"

The answer became evident shortly thereafter in 1992 when the "for sale" sign went up in front of the two-story house at 1211 East Main Street, right next door to the house that burned down. This house would be renovated to make a shelter for mothers with preschool children. The now vacant

1211 E. Main St.
First house for women's ministry.

Mayor Harry Rodenhiezer cuts the ribbon for the grand opening of The Opportunity Place!

lot left by the fire provided the much-needed outdoor space for a playground area for the children that would soon fill the house.

"The Lord made the money available when the opportunity was there," said Gail.

The new ministry would also provide opportunities for counseling, life skills training, education, and rehabilitation for women. These many opportunities translated into the first name for the women's ministry: "The Opportunity Place."

"At one point I was so hungry, I got food out of a dumpster. It made me feel less than human."

— Sharon

By the time most women get to the Durham Rescue Mission, just about everyone in their lives has given up on them, including themselves. Women with children are especially vulnerable on the streets. The Mission is a respite from the unimaginable storm which has led them to desperate measures like fishing food out of fast food dumpsters or sleeping in abandoned cars.

"I was choked and punched repeatedly." *— Robin*

"Trapped and worthless were my first thoughts each morning." *— Tonia*

They may have left an abusive relationship with nowhere to go. For others, family members refuse to take one more chance on them, just to have them go back to drugs or prostitution. Whatever the reasons, employers are tired of excuses; friends are long gone.

Most of the women, who Sal Nolfo, Ph.D., counsels at the Durham Rescue Mission, have shed any societal boundaries.

On the street, they were free to do what they wanted, and they also broke whatever rule they needed to in order to survive. At the Mission, they enter the women's ministry where Nolfo serves as director, and his wife Marge is

Dr. Sal Nolfo

a computer and Bible instructor. Although homeless and desperate, some women are reluctant to give up their "freedom" for a structured environment.

"If there's a locomotive coming down a hill, is the train freer when it's on the track coming down or when it's off the track coming down?" Nolfo might ask them. The women generally concede the train is freer on the track because when it's off the track, it may hit a tree. It might veer off onto an uneven path which will slow it down considerably and make the trip unsteady or unsafe. They can see the connection he draws to their own lives.

In Nolfo's illustration, the track is the Bible, which gives guidelines for life. Yet, Nolfo continues, it helps smooth the way to a person's desired destination.

"If you want to do it your way, outside the confines of God's Word, that's going to be an awfully bumpy road. You may even crash and burn," Nolfo said.

Because these women have experienced devastating losses and traversed some very bumpy terrain in life, often the idea of a new course of action appeals to them and they will at least listen to how biblical principles help get people back on track.

It is a consuming profession, being a counselor at a homeless shelter, and it is not something Nolfo intended to do full time at all. Like so many others who start volunteering at the Mission, once he started, he could not ignore the overwhelming needs or the fact that he could help. The job chose him.

Instead of the leisurely retirement he was anticipating after selling off his two pest control businesses in nearby Garner, Nolfo took a much more demanding job than he had ever had. The physically and emotionally draining aspect of the work of delving into people's emotions is far outweighed by the fulfillment of seeing lives changed, he said.

A certified family and marital counselor, Nolfo and his wife Marge oversee the women and children's ministry as a team. Marge heads up the 12-month computer training program in which the women can receive certification in various Microsoft programs, including Word, Excel, Power-Point, Access, Outlook, and Windows.

The training also includes a course basic medical terminology because Durham is known as the City of Medicine, and 30 percent of the jobs are related to the medical field.

The training leads to better paying jobs that often double the salary they could earn as an unskilled laborer earning minimum wage. The Mission helps connect their graduates to available jobs at area companies. In order to have reliable transportation to these jobs, the Mission, which accepts donated vehicles from the community, sells those cars to the mothers at a greatly reduced price from market value.

Both Sal and Marge were originally volunteers at the Mission. Neither expected their volunteering to lead them into full-time mission work. Within a month of starting, just as Nolfo was phasing out his lucrative pest control business, Ernie asked him to come on board full time, and he started in February 2003.

"He caught me right at the right time, I guess," said Nolfo, who smiled and added he's working twice as hard and earning half as much as he did as a businessman.

"But when a person comes to you and says 'I'm back on

cocaine,' you can open the Bible to offer hope to that person. That definitely negates anything you'd complain about here."

Nolfo sees great hopelessness in the women when they arrive. In their desperation, they have turned to any number of "solutions" the world offers and found themselves so much farther from hope with their problems compounded by drugs, alcohol, and destructive behaviors like prostitution.

Nolfo said he was attracted to the Mission's unique long-term commitment to offering practical Bible-based counseling instead of simply providing temporary housing.

Bible study is daily, although no one is required to become a Christian. The first class of the day consists of a devotional in which the women learn how to gain life skills through building a biblical foundation. From budgeting money to raising children to staying drug-free, many women who enter the program are surprised that every aspect of their disorganized lives has a scriptural remedy.

The strongest emphasis of the program is biblical counseling because no matter how many computer or life skills they succeed at learning, if their hearts are not changed, the old patterns will re-emerge, Nolfo said.

"If an individual comes in here as a drunkard, they've lost everything—their marriage, their home. The state's got the children. The Bible says people resort to alcohol as an escape from something," Nolfo explained. "In counseling, we really dig."

Often, the women are traumatized by having been abused, physically or sexually by a father or other family member. Or a spouse may have committed suicide. Typically, the guilt, anger, depression, or bitterness they are trying to alleviate with drugs or alcohol could be caused by abandonment, the death of a spouse or a child, or they are overwhelmed with guilt because they have had one or more abortions, Nolfo said.

"That really takes a toll on a person. Address the hard issues and the symptoms go away," Nolfo said. After listening carefully to a new resident's specific situation, Nolfo finds scripture to explain why their emotional reactions to their situations don't work for them.

Many of these women have been indoctrinated with the world view that says, "If it feels right, do it," but God wants us to disregard those desires and do what is right, Marge said.

With her undergraduate degree in psychology and a minor in criminology from Meredith College in Raleigh, Marge Nolfo is uniquely suited to teach and counsel this special population. For the great majority of residents, it is their first exposure to using computers, and generally 50 percent have not completed high school. In 2004, the Mission began receiving help from Durham Technical Community College on this front. Instructors teach classes at the Mission that help residents obtain their General Equivalency Diploma.

Another obstacle to educational advancement for the women, Marge said, is the pervasive use of drugs. Often they have only been able to work in low-paying, menial jobs to get by and to feed themselves and their drug habits.

Add in teen pregnancies and other life-altering poor choices during their rebellious teen years and the women who wind up at the Mission have often spent 20 years in and out of social services. The average age of women checking into the Mission is between 35 and 40, but ranges from 18 on up.

At first, when they arrive at the Mission, Marge explains to each of them that they are on a 30-day restriction, under which they are monitored. With drugs being a prevalent problem among the women, the 30-day period at least keeps them clean so they can begin to think clearly.

Since addiction comes in many forms, the women are also strictly forbidden to fraternize with men. Many have a history of "revolving men" or of prostitution.

"Sometimes they have been addicted for so long, they think all they need is a man," Marge said. The restrictions keep them from going back out on the street.

Some women complain that the rules are too strict in the beginning, but soon realize the rules are there for their protection and guidance.

Chapter 18
DAUGHTER'S HEARING RESTORED AS MOTHER LEARNS TO LISTEN

*T*here is no way to calculate what the Mission has done for the women who have come for help. Examples like Tina Hogan, though, demonstrate how it can help.

She lived on her own since she was 16 years old.

"When I was only 16 years old, my own mother's live-in boyfriend was an alcoholic. Mother worked second shift, and that meant that I was alone with him at nights. One night he pushed me down on the bed – and I was able to push him off of me. I ran to my room. When I finally got the courage to tell my mom, she did not believe me. That left me feeling afraid. I was hurt, scared and angry all at the same time," Tina recalled.

That's when she decided she couldn't stay where she didn't feel safe. She slept at friends' houses, and even stayed with one of her teachers for a while in order to earn her high school diploma.

"Sometimes I would have to walk four miles to get to school. I was working at a pizza restaurant and many times I would not get off until 2 a.m. I had the constant worry of where I would sleep tomorrow," she said.

But she graduated on time and even had a perfect score in her senior English class.

Right after graduation, she got married and soon had a baby girl, named Regina.

"My marriage was rocky from the beginning," she said, and eventually it fell apart.

After she left her husband, she moved from a campground to motels, where there were never adequate cooking facilities.

"We lived off of bread, cheese, and sometimes we would eat beef stew directly out of the can. Then, when it got to the point that I paid the last bit of rent in pennies, I knew I had hit rock bottom," she said.

"When the following week rolled around, I had no more money and once again, we were on the move. My ex-husband was stalking me. I remember one night that I sent Regina away, and I slept under a bridge to keep him from finding me."

In June of 1996, she was 21, and Regina was 2 ½. Tina was concerned that Regina wasn't talking yet. The toddler was only making grunting noises, but Tina had too many other problems to cope with and no money to see a doctor.

In the six months since she had left her husband, they had moved 13 times. This was not a new state of affairs, as since Regina was born, they had moved 25 times.

The stress was mounting. She drank to get relief. She finally decided she was going to quit her job as a waitress at Shoney's and join some friends to travel state to state building mausoleums.

"It pays better than being a waitress," she shrugged, explaining the unlikely plan. Her group of friends, including her daughter, planned to travel from city to city in a van while they worked in their unusual itinerant jobs.

Before she left for this questionable new employment opportunity, she put on the only dress she owned and walked to Fellowship Baptist Church in Durham to bid farewell to some friends.

Those friends encouraged her to switch gears and instead go get help at the Mission. She packed up all their meager belongings in a laundry basket and headed to the Mission.

"That night, I was staying at the Durham Rescue Mission," she said. "I did not want to take my daughter to a shelter. I thought that would be the worst place I could take her. I thought building mausoleums would be better than going to a dirty, smelly shelter.

Tina and Regina Hogan found a safe and stable home at the mission after years of struggling and moving 25 times in 2½ years.

"When I got to the Mission, I was surprised by what I found. The house was clean, bright, and cheerful. After years of struggling to keep a roof over our heads, Regina now had her own room, and I had mine."

Instead of being the dead end she thought it would be, it turned out to be the end of a vicious cycle that had overtaken her life. It was the hand-up she needed to get her daughter into a stable environment.

"It's not a hand-out. You have to do the work."

It was also a chance to pay attention to Regina's needs, and find out why she wasn't talking yet at 2 ½ years old.

The Mission arranged for Regina to see a doctor, who determined the little girl had lost 60 percent of her hearing in one ear, and 40 percent in the other.

"The doctor explained it to me that it was like she was under water, so everything she heard was muffled and when she tried to talk, she repeated sounds that she heard. Even though she was 2½, developmentally, she was on the level of a 9-month-old.

"On November 1st, 1996, doctors put tubes in her ears,

Regina Hogan is now a happy 4th grader and is the joy of her mother's life.

and it was like she was hearing things for the first time," Hogan said.

After Regina got the tubes, she started speech therapy.

"It's like she found the on-button, and I've been looking for the off-button ever since," her mother laughed.

"I was 21, and had not been to the doctor in two years, because from the time I was 15, up until I was 19, doctors said I had cancerous cells. I was scared to go back to the doctor. I thought it was better to ignore it," Hogan said.

"While at the Mission, I started going to the doctor as well. I found out that I had asthma, but praise the Lord no sign of cancer," Hogan said.

Tina Hogan is really happy to have a stable job working for Hank Scherich at Measurement, Inc.

The Durham Rescue Mission, she said, not only helped the pair get appropriate medical care, but provided a solid foundation of biblical instruction, a safe place to live, hot meals, clean clothing, and valuable vocational skills.

"On March 28th, 1997, I graduated from their women's program, and I have not worked a minimum wage job since! I got a job in Research Triangle Park. I soldered, debugged, and trouble-shot circuit boards!"

Then, when the economy hit a downturn, she was laid off. The Mission was able to help her find another job almost immediately with Measurement Inc. The company owner, and now Durham Chamber of Commerce President, Henry "Hank" Scherich, gave her the job through Temps to the Rescue. Through that experience, she was hired on as a permanent employee.  The Mission also gave her a Toyota Camry that had been donated, so she would have dependable transportation and, thus, a better chance of staying employed.

"I thank God the Mission was there to help me in my time of need," said Hogan, after living independently for five years since leaving the Mission.

"Before the Durham Rescue Mission, it was *all* I could do just to get through the day. I did not even know where we would live from day to day," she said.

"Yes, at one time, I thought going to the Durham Rescue Mission was the worst place I could go. But now I know it was the best place that I could have ever gone. I want to thank the staff of the Durham Rescue Mission and the supporters of the Mission for giving my daughter and me a helping hand up in our time of need. They truly offer a hand-up, not a hand-out, like they say. A hand-up can last a lifetime."

Chapter 19
A WOMAN'S YEAR

With plans for opening the Mission's new Home for Single Women in the final stages and Bethany's wedding just a couple weeks away, Gail was consumed with last minute details for both major events in August of 1998.

As she sat in her office discussing an annual personnel evaluation with one of the staff members, a glance at the clock startled her into the realization that she had five minutes to get to a doctor's appointment for her annual physical exam.

It crossed her mind to reschedule, but something made her jump up and race to the appointment. Blessed with good health all her life, the first unexpected inkling that something was amiss came with a phone call from the doctor's office the next day and a request for her to come in to re-take her mammogram. The nurse told her in 80 percent of women who must have a follow-up mammogram, no tumors are found, so it wasn't necessarily a big deal. That the prestigious Duke University Hospital wanted her in the very next day to repeat the exam was a bit disconcerting, though.

The next day turned into what seemed an endless series of mammograms and ultrasounds taken from every angle. Finally, the radiologist took her into a room to show her the irregular mass in the area they were concerned about.

"Mrs. Mills, there's no doubt in my mind that you've got breast cancer," he told her.

She was quickly scheduled to have a tissue sample taken,

but with the Labor Day weekend upon them, it took several interminable days to get the biopsy results. When they did come, they confirmed what the radiologist had suspected.

Gail told the children first and decided to wait until after Bethany's wedding and honeymoon to have the recommended surgery.

"The wedding was absolutely beautiful. Ernie helped perform the ceremony and shared the vows. Everybody just rallied around me to help with the wedding preparations. They treated me like I couldn't do anything," Gail said.

Her son-in-law's mother, Mary Stroup, who had undergone a mastectomy, gave Gail a teddy bear as a sign of comfort and to make her smile. "To this day, I have that little stuffed bear in my guest bedroom."

The cancer was in the early stages, but Gail chose a mastectomy over a lumpectomy so that she could avoid radiation treatment. One of the 10 lymph nodes that were removed during the surgery was also cancerous. That meant she would have to go through chemotherapy.

She sought three different opinions, in hopes of avoiding chemotherapy, but all three told her it was unavoidable. Dr. Robert Stewart, her primary care physician at the time, researched her options thoroughly. He told her: "Gail, we want to give you every percentage point we can to defeat this cancer and that includes chemo,'" Gail recalled.

As a Christian, Stewart, who later went on to become head of the student clinic at Southeastern Baptist Theological Seminary in nearby Wake Forest, was not just their trusted physician but a trusted friend and fellow believer.

"Ernie and I went to him and he prayed with us," Gail said.

Tests indicated her tumor contained a particularly aggressive Her2neu protein, which can prove fatal even if caught in the early stages of breast cancer.

Later, after testing became more sophisticated, she would discover it was not present in her cancer, but she thinks there were lessons she was supposed to learn from having the chemotherapy.

"One of the lessons was that God could take care of me. Before I took the chemo drugs, they had to tell me all the side effects. I was reading about possible side effects, and Ernie came in the room to find me just weeping. He said, 'You need to put that stuff up,'" Gail said.

"When you get news like that, you're just numb," Ernie said. "It's something you never expect to happen, especially when you see someone you love so dearly and see the anguish in her heart and her mind, not knowing what the outcome will be."

Gail remembers the fear that she brought to the Lord as she found herself spending all her time doing research on her condition and the potential side effects of each alternative treatment.

"Lord, your Word says you do not give us a spirit of fear. I don't know why I'm so scared. If I die, I'm going to be with you in heaven. I don't understand where this fear is coming from," she prayed. She realized her focus was on the cancer and the chemo and not on Christ.

"I got on my knees and I asked God to forgive me. Seek the Lord, seek his face continually was the Bible verse from First Chronicles that comforted me. The Lord did relieve my fear once my focus was on Him—but I still had that horrible dread of going in that treatment room every three weeks."

What gave her the daily strength she needed after that was reading the Bible and the gentle attention of Ernie.

"He was just so tender and loving and reassuring, saying that it's not my body he loves, it's me," she said. He juiced 50 pounds of carrots a week for her to stay on the Hallelujah Diet; a juicing diet that she says strengthened her body to tolerate the chemotherapy treatments.

Ernie also helped her cut off what remained of her hair when it began to fall out in clumps. "That is

Gail's hair did grow back after the chemo treatments!

the sorriest hair cut I ever had," she laughed, recalling how tormented she was when her hair, eyebrows, and eyelashes started falling out. But, she smiled; at least she didn't have to shave her legs.

She continued to work at the Mission, but Ernie would insist that she lie down and rest at midday.

"If I did not, he came looking for me," she said.

He also prayed with her.

That anxious morning of her first chemotherapy treatment, the couple was reading Proverbs 30 before preparing to go to the hospital. They came to Verse 5. "Every word of God is pure: He is a shield unto them that put their trust in Him."

Ernie excitedly slapped the table with his hand. He looked up and said, "We're going to ask God to put a shield about your body to protect you from the side effects of the chemo."

As if in confirmation, just as Ernie flipped on the radio to catch the weather report, a woman's voice boldly sang, "He is my strength and shield!"

"We knew God was confirming this," Gail said.

During that first treatment, Gail looked down at her

hand where the intravenous needle was inserted and noticed a little bubbling beneath the skin. She asked the nurse
what was happening, and the nurse immediately yanked
the line out.

The vein had blown and the Adriamyacin, a caustic
chemo drug, was beginning to bubble beneath her skin.
When she went for a checkup with the doctor three weeks
later, he asked what the red mark was on the back of her
hand. When she told him, he was amazed that she did not
have a deep ulcer because the drug is so strong. That, she
said, was further confirmation that God was protecting her
body from the assault of chemo treatments. She never experienced nausea or had to miss a treatment due to low white
blood cell count.

She also learned that caring for others is the best way to
care for yourself.

"God showed me that I needed to think of others instead
of dwelling on what was going on in my life and being so
consumed with it," she said. She made it a point of sending
cards to anyone on the prayer list in the church bulletin and
making sure she rejoiced with friends about the celebra-
tions in their lives.

"That really helped me," she said.

"It gives you a new perspective on life. So many things
that seem so big, I look at them now and say, in the big picture, are they really important? People will ask what if this
cancer comes back. But that can be answered with, 'God is
still in control. God has promised to give us grace and mercy, and His mercies are fresh and new every day.'"

Ernie said the lessons of that experience were for both
of them.

"When we came back from our fear and focused our
attention on the sufficiency of God, we were comforted

knowing that nothing takes Him by surprise. God is able to work it out for His glory and good. That's when it seemed like He started giving us the victory," Ernie said. "It's not that it would be exactly what we wanted it to be, but it's according to His will."

At the time, the news was devastating to everyone at the Mission. Rev. Tart thought for sure they should just halt their plans to open the new single women's shelter.

Gail would not hear of it.

"No, this is God's ministry," she said.

The Home for Single Women opened in November of 1998, right on schedule, and Gail has been cancer free since receiving those dreaded cancer treatments.

Rocky Shelton could be called an unlikely missionary. He is as surprised as anyone. A debilitating stutter acquired as a boy might have been enough to keep another man from seeking out public speaking engagements. His checkered past of drug addiction, armed robbery, and prison might have deterred another man from such a calling.

But it is because of those very things that Shelton feels the Lord has given him a boldness to tell his own traumatic story. It is a cautionary tale given more credence through his experience. Those awful experiences are why he feels an urgency to share the Gospel that transformed his life and pulled him from such a destructive path.

A week-long visit to the Durham Rescue Mission in 1999 with his church group convinced Shelton he had been sent there for a specific reason. In fact, right in the middle of the revival, while singing to the residents, he turned to Ernie Mills and told him in front of everyone that he was going to start a mission just like this one in his hometown of Shelby, North Carolina.

Never one to miss an opportunity, that single spontaneous pronouncement was enough for Ernie to take action. He took up a collection and, at the end of the revival, handed Rocky an envelope with $1,000 to help get him started.

It wasn't long before Rocky was leasing a building from his home church, Faith Baptist Church in Shelby, where he headed the prison ministry to the nearby Cleveland Correctional Center. He founded Crossroads Rescue Mission. With the prison as a backdrop, Rocky felt called to counsel men like himself before they wind up incarcerated.

He knew from personal experience that it is not a pleasant place to be.

In 1985, 30-year-old Shelton was a desperate drunk and cocaine addict. His wife had finally had enough and left him. He worked odd jobs at the local cotton mills but mostly gambled and hustled pool to pay for his next fix. "I was awful," Shelton sums up.

As a youngster, his moral but stern father had reprimanded him for stuttering; only making matters worse. His namesake was boxing champ Rocky Marciano, whom his father was watching pound someone when his mother was in the hospital delivery room. To be sure, young Rocky had his share of fights in school. Mostly they started when someone would make fun of him if he had to read aloud or speak in class. His response for the constant teasing about his speech impediment was always with his fists.

He dropped out of high school three months shy of graduation because his daddy made him marry the girl he'd gotten pregnant. The teenage marriage ended after his stint in the military when, as he put it, they both had done their own thing because they weren't in love.

Looking back now, he still can't believe he sunk as low as he did. He held up a pharmacy at gunpoint in 1985, forcing customers to lie down on the floor as he committed the crime. That got him 10 years for kidnapping and armed robbery at Cleveland Correctional Center. Perhaps if he had known what that place was like, he would have thought twice about committing the crime.

"It's a rough camp," said Shelton, who nonetheless returns there frequently, albeit for an entirely different reason. He still shivers at the guns pointed at the inmates daily and the lack of privacy and dignity, with open showers and toilets.

According to the information on its website, the medium security prison hasn't changed much since it was built as a field camp in the 1930s to house inmates who worked building roads. The prison's original housing units are still in use today.

Shelton would come to realize that what brought him to that bleak place and brought him to rock bottom also brought him his salvation.

"I wasn't raised in church, but my wife Deborah had got saved three years earlier. We was at war! I was doing drugs and drinking. We had been separated for eight months, and she told me 'I don't want to see you no more.'"

When he got to jail, though, Deborah figured she'd try one more time to reach him since she had a captive audience. "You've tried everything else, why don't you try the Lord," she told him as she handed him a Bible.

As he read in Isaiah 53, a chapter which describes the lamb to the slaughter, it was the first time he'd ever considered that the Lord had sent Christ to die for him.

Rocky and Deborah Shelton started the Crossroads Rescue Mission in Shelby, NC. God has mightly used them to help the homeless and addicted.

"I said, 'If you save my soul tonight, Lord, everything I do will be for you.'"

True to his word, after serving three years at Cleveland, he was paroled and did 18 months of community service, working for the Red Cross every week. He started his own roof repair and home improvement business and immediately joined a church and began singing in the choir.

Soon thereafter, long-time preacher B.L. Queen, who'd been visiting the prison for 30 years, asked the former inmate to join him in his prison ministry. Shelton eagerly accepted because he said he knew what the men were going through. He applied to the prison for permission but was turned down repeatedly because he had not been out of prison long enough. After five years of asking, he finally got the green light. When Pastor Queen died in 1996, the church asked Shelton to become director of the prison ministry.

"I just about had a spell," exclaims Shelton about his response to the request.

He has a kinship with the inmates, even though he can hardly relate to the person who held up a pharmacy at gunpoint so long ago.

"Everybody who knew of it would have never thought that I would have done anything like that because that wasn't my nature. It wasn't my personality. But when you get under the influence of drugs and alcohol, you're liable to do anything. You've given your consciousness over to a foreign substance and it's controlling you. I believe that all illegal drugs and alcohol are of the devil," he said.

Shelton said the inmates listen to him because of their shared experiences.

"They cry and say 'Amen' at what I say. I can get through," Shelton said. It gives him hope for the men. As devastating as his criminal past was, he is grateful for it because without that brokenness, he could not have accepted the Lord's grace.

In 2004, after being married for 25 years, Shelton is still in awe of the woman who stayed by his side through his prison term and remains supportive of his ministry.

"Once I got saved, never once in all those years has she mentioned my past," Shelton confided.

It is the same emotion-filled reverence with which he talks about his children. He has a good relationship with his daughter from his first teenage marriage. One of his sons took over the family business, and when his other son graduated from business school, he became development director for Crossroads Rescue Mission.

"If you were a drunk and you couldn't keep $20 a week in your pocket and you see the Lord bless your life and your children's lives, it's more than you can bear," he explains. "It's been a wonderful life.

"Twenty years ago, if anyone would have told me that I would ever be doing anything for the Lord, I'd have cussed him out and run him off."

He believes the Lord wants him to help others who have been through what he has been through. He also believes he's here to help people headed in that direction to learn that their story does not have to be like his. He knows he was sent to the Durham Rescue Mission to be inspired about how to go about it.

"A week of sleeping with them and eating with them and seeing them in classes showed me that it was exactly what the Lord wanted in Shelby."

The Crossroads Rescue Mission usually caters to drug addicts and alcoholics, and Shelton proudly announced one of the men who was saved at the mission graduated from a Bible college in 2004 and became assistant youth pastor at a local church.

Had it not been for Ernie Mills and the inspiration of the Durham Rescue Mission, Shelton isn't sure that would have all come about.

"They are good people who want to see lives changed."

*I*t doesn't take much to make Walter Cole smile these days, a dramatic example of how a person can change at the Mission. His warmth is one of the reasons he was given the responsibility of being a counselor at the mission.

For most of his life, however, Cole did not have much to smile about.

Locked up in prison, doing hard time for 22 years and nine months, much of it in maximum security, Cole invariably adopted a miserable attitude and felt that he was being taken advantage of. Even before he got to prison, a wall of resentment surrounded his upbringing in rural Guilford County, North Carolina.

At age 24, he robbed a local convenience store at gunpoint in a heroin haze. As he puts it, "I robbed the wrong people," so instead of the seven year sentence he might have expected, he got the most severe, 25 years for armed robbery.

But, he doesn't make excuses. He did the crime, and, he says: "I was using heroin because that's what I wanted to do." He discovered the drug during a stint in the military at a young age. He had been drinking alcohol since age 14 and experimented with marijuana. Married at 18, his wife divorced him when he got sent up for the robbery.

With a military efficiency, Cole recounts the tale that brought him to the Durham Rescue Mission in 2002.

In the early years of his prison tenure, he could see the

parole board was stacked against him ever getting out early, so he started plotting his escape. He actually did escape -- twice, but that just got more years added on to his sentence and landed him in maximum security, where the only time he was let out of his cell was Wednesday mornings.

Once he earned his way out of that, he was allowed to operate the printing press, where the inmates made license plates and road signs.

Finally released in 1994, perhaps predictably, the first place he headed was to find a dealer. Crack cocaine then seized his life, and he started a cycle of rehab and relapses that lasted eight years. In 2001, during a dry spell, he got married, but was back in rehab the following year.

"I had been through anger management, stress management, every program they have. I was thoroughly confused," he says. He was also tired of the ceaseless cycle that always seemed to lead to the same unpleasant place. In 2002, while being evaluated for self-destructive mental health issues, a screener noted that he seemed to have tried every program the state had, to no avail.

Then, to his surprise, she asked him if he had ever tried God.

Cole laughed bitterly and replied, "Ma'am, I forgot about God a long time ago."

He soon learned God had never forgotten about him.

The woman asked if he would be willing to try something different since he obviously had no mental illness. Sick of the spiral cycle of getting clean and holding a job for a few months, only to lose it to crack, Cole agreed.

She told him about the Durham Rescue Mission and its recovery program for alcoholics and drug addicts.

At the mission barely two months, Cole brokenly opened his heart to Jesus and surrendered himself to the Lord. For the first time in his entire life, he could plainly see that there were people who wanted to help him.

"The first year I was here, I was really convinced that these people have got to be real," he said, referring to Ernie and Gail Mills.

"Their grandson was a baby, and they were here Christmas morning giving out presents. Here, instead of home with the baby!" Cole said.

"I had always been in programs, but I was just waiting to get out and go get high. This place has really helped me. They gave me an opportunity. This is a place of refuge, where I could gather my thoughts. There are people out here that do love you. They teach you that God loves you. I knew about the crucifixion, but I didn't know it involved me."

Cole said that all his life, even in prison, he wanted to help people. He occasionally did help a few, but he could never help himself. "And I always got caught up in the feeling that I was being taken advantage of."

Now, it's different, and his own experience helps him get through to some of the hard cases who walk through

Walter Cole is so proud to have his family back together after years of separation.

the door. "Today I smile, when I never did smile. I'm back with my wife, Leola. I'm in Cedar Grove Bible College, taking Bible courses. I'm a Christian counselor. I believe in my heart that God was preparing me for what I'm doing right now. He takes all the bad and turns it to good. It was a lot of suffering, a lot of pain, but I realize also that I brought it on myself. The mission helped me deal with that."

In 2004, after some minimum security prison inmates raised $500 for the Mission from washing cars, two of them were brought to the Mission to deliver the donation.

As Ernie accepted the check and learned they were still inmates, he introduced them to Cole. After they spoke with him for a while, they asked if he would come to speak at the prison, and arrangements were made.

Just before Christmas, Cole told the inmates he knew how they were feeling, facing Christmas in prison, because he'd done it 22 times. But, he said, Christ had made a difference in his life and the Lord could change their lives, too.

The prisoners responded with a standing ovation.

Chapter 22
MISSION IS A "WARM SHELTER"— LITERALLY

*D*ennis Bynum had no intention of ever coming to the Durham Rescue Mission. He must have passed the mission a thousand times in his dispossessed meanderings about town. He knew about the rules and the religion, and that was enough to keep him away.

Regulations and restrictions on his freedom were not what he wanted. And face it, at age 38, he was as free as a person can get. Without home or family, he had no responsibilities, nothing to tie him down. Well, that's if you didn't count his son. But the boy lived with his mother, a woman Bynum never married. She would take good care of their son, so he tried not to dwell on that too much.

He also knew the Durham Rescue Mission wouldn't let him go out and work right away, and the lack of income might interfere with his crack habit. That definitely wasn't for him. So, when a massive ice storm forced him to take refuge, he opted for an overnight shelter downtown to get out its relentless path.

Millions lost electricity in the devastating ice storm of 2002 which swept the southeast United States. Power lines weighed down with heavy ice snapped by the thousands. When the downtown shelter lost its heat, the temperature dropped precipitously inside. With no heat, the crowded and frigid shelter felt unbearable to this man who had isolated himself from as much human contact as possible.

Ernie and Gail stopped by the downtown shelter to drop off a large pot of hot homemade soup and to invite anyone at the freezing shelter to come over to the Mission where it was warm, because they heated with a wood stove.

In bitter weather, when the temperature dips danger-ously, the Durham Rescue Mission institutes "Operation Warm Shelter," making sweeps of the community in all the likely places—under bridges or in abandoned buildings—anywhere someone might freeze to death exposed to the elements. Local law enforcement officials drop off anyone they find at the Mission as well.

Mission workers hand out flyers inviting the homeless to come in from the cold. The mission is always packed dur-ing severe weather. In that 2002 ice storm, a record number of 202 men, women and children spent the night.

Storm stories abound about the life-saving program. One memorable incident happened in 1996, when another severe winter storm brought Silas Monroe in from the cold—close to hypothermia, by all accounts. A homeless alcoholic, the 38-year-old wandered the streets until he collapsed.

There was a flyer in his pocket that a Mission worker had given him earlier in the day and found by the Durham police officer who scraped the ice-encrusted man from the sidewalk where he lay. She brought him to the mission to thaw out, and literally saved his life.

In 2002, during the life-threatening ice storm, Bynum thought for a while about the invitation from the Durham Rescue Mission. Chilled to the bone sitting in that cold shel-ter, he thought about the heat and the hot meal offered by the Mission. After a few hours of shivering, Bynum decid-ed, rules or not, he had to get warm. The decision changed his life.

He braved the ice storm and walked to the Mission, where he was greeted by a supervisor named Charles Min-nifield, who asked him about himself and told him his own story. Minnifield told him about the Victory Program for men.

Bynum told him he was just there for the hot coffee and a meal while he waited out the storm, but Minnifield encouraged him to think about staying and joining the program.

Bynum said he had been to a revival downtown a couple of years before and had accepted Jesus as his savior, but, he backslid into crack. He promised Minnifield he'd pray about it and sleep on it before he made the decision to leave.

"It was the best sleep I had in months," even though he was on a cot in the crowded dining room.

"God did the changing, there's no doubt in my mind about that. He spoke to my heart that night. This is where he wanted me to be. I was struggling. I was ready to get off the streets. I was fed up and tired of that lifestyle," Bynum recalled.

The intense Bible-based training he received at the Mission taught him he could make good decisions, he said.

"I can think better. My head's a lot clearer. I take care of my responsibilities. I see myself as being a lot better Christian."

Before, without that daily practical foundation, he lost his way, and is realistic about knowing he needs that support.

"Temptations come. Giving into them is not the easy way, though. From experience, I know it's a copout. It doesn't work at all. All you do is cause yourself more heartache. As soon as those thoughts pop up, I'll go to something else. By learning what I've learned already, I can quote scripture right off the top of my head," Bynum said.

Going to the Mission changed his life in all kinds of ways, not the least of which was a newfound determination to be part of his son's life. Another was meeting Tracy

Criss.

After 20 years of drug use, and two children out of wed-lock, Criss was back at the Mission for a second time after trying to go out on her own. Growing up in Durham, she attended a local African Methodist Episcopal Zion Church, which had what she called a "fire and brimstone" approach to the Gospel, something she never quite connected with.

Rebellious as a teen, she got into drugs early, but was always able to hold down a good job – until the drugs took complete control of her life. Then, in October of 2000, she gave birth to little Mario at Duke University Medical Center.

When nurses asked her about her medical history, she answered truthfully about her drug use—that she had smoked crack that very night.

A blood test showed both mother and infant tested positive for crack, so social services stepped in and took custody of Mario. She had been in denial about the pregnancy, and had hidden it from all her relatives and friends. Once she heard his cry, though, she realized she did not want to repeat what had happened with her first child. Her parents were caring for her daughter, because, in her words, "I preferred cocaine over motherhood."

A hospital social worker suggested she try the Mission because she didn't even have diapers or a place to stay for the child, and she would need stability to get her baby boy back. After a week at the Mission, by establishing that she would be under supervision and would be able to provide a safe environment for the baby, she was granted physical custody.

By staying clean and staying at the Mission, she was also able to regain full legal custody of the healthy little boy. She soon felt strong enough to go out on her own, got an apartment, and a job.

By February of 2004, however, she had relapsed and was back at the Mission, this time with a sincere desire to get help. Once back, she finally heard what she needed to hear.

"I was always told I was an addict. Mr. Sal (Nolfo) taught me I'm not an addict until I pick up. If I'm not using, then I'm not addicted—and it's my choice," Criss said. "It was only the Lord that saved me because I know I should be dead," she said.

Later in 2004, at a staff appreciation dinner, Bynum gave his testimony, and Criss heard something that touched her heart in a new way.

"He cried and said he hit rock bottom, and the rock that he fell on was Jesus Christ," Criss said.

Fraternization is forbidden between unmarried male and female residents of the Mission, who are housed in different places. One day, Criss saw Bynum at the local grocery store, where she congratulated him on his graduation from the Victory Program.

He didn't know her, but he liked her immediately, and the pair decided to make a clandestine date in the nearby park. They were found out and placed on restriction. Since both had been through the Victory Program, they asked for permission to date each other, and eventually it was granted.

"It's biblical dating. There's no touching, no kissing. We talked. I had never done that before," Criss said. Getting to know each other and learning each other's history taught her an important lesson.

"The Lord took us through all of this. We weren't ready for each other 20 years ago. I just saw myself as a user, an abuser, a victim—because I put myself in that position," Criss said. The Mission helped her find out she was much more.

If he had not come to the Mission, "I would probably be dead," Bynum echoed Chriss's sentiments. "On the street out there, it's real cruel. It's real dangerous."

What does he have to say about Ernie and Gail Mills?

"Oh, that's my mom and my dad," smiles Bynum. "They are wonderful folks."

In fact, when his mother couldn't make it to his and Tracy's wedding in the Mission chapel in September of 2004—the first marriage between mission residents—Gail stood in for her that day. The couple is now independent, with their own apartment and steady jobs.

What a blessing to have Dennis and Tracy Bynum return to the Mission as voluteers. They helped us give away 2,300 backpacks to needy children at our annual "Back to School" party!

Gail Mills smiles as she describes the enthusiastic welcome she and Ernie invariably receive at City Hall.

"Public officials are always glad to see us because they know we're not there asking for money," she laughs. First and foremost, the mission of the Mission is to save lost souls and share the Gospel, and the couple is happily unrepentant about standing firm in that commitment. The Mission doesn't accept government money because it will not compromise on sharing the love of Christ with those who are hurting. Not that he needs evidence, but Ernie has seen many lives transformed when people commit their lives to the Lord.

Ernie has gone so far as to return a $10,000 government grant which a local legislator applied for without telling the Mission. Though touched by the gesture, Ernie believes the separation he keeps from government funding has actually benefited the growth of the Mission.

Although the Mission doesn't measure its success in financial terms, and never accepts government funding, it prepares an annual report for government officials as a friendly reminder of the value the Mission adds to the community.

Those figures added up to nearly $3.2 million for 2004, which is a bargain basement estimate considering it values one of the 181,111 meals they served at only $5 each, and one of the 58,969 individual nights of lodging at only $15.

As a certified Microsoft testing facility, the $15 per hour

of vocational training is also probably a bit conservative, but the numbers are only used to illustrate a point. The value of the Microsoft training and medical terminology classes for the women in the Mission's program has value far beyond the certificates the women can receive or even the jobs they get. Not only do they learn that people are willing to help them, they have their own sense of accomplishment about learning at such a high level.

The Mission also uses a conservative estimate of $30 per hour for counseling services, which would have amounted to $248,690 in 2004.

The community benefits as much as the individuals who are able to support themselves with their newly learned skills.

The Mission also gave out 200,408 items of clothing, including winter coats to the needy in Durham in 2004. It is a cycle that enriches the community by showing how much the public cares by donating those much needed items in the first place.

In this regard, the mission is far more than a monetary plus or minus sign on the balance sheet of the city.

As bold as Ernie and Gail are in sharing their belief in Jesus Christ as Lord and Savior, support for the Mission goes well beyond the Christian community. The Mission has succeeded in community outreach in ways no government agencies have in Durham. The impact cuts across all socio-economic barriers.

The business community has rallied around the Mission. Downtown Durham Rotary Club even honored Ernie with its coveted Paul Harris Award, unprecedented for a non-member.

While the majority of the Mission's budget is met by small, individual donations, corporations large and small have adopted it as a civic improvement project. Glaxo-SmithKline established a scholarship endowment for the Mission which will total $250,000 to be used for job training after residents graduate from the Victory Program.

With the Mission's plans to triple the size of its program for homeless women and children, Verizon and the Mary Duke Biddle Foundation have provided a grant to include web page design as well.

Sometimes the outpouring of generosity even stuns these veterans of giving and receiving kindness. From individuals to churches to corporations to the unlikeliest of donors, people respond with a common desire to help others.

The Mission has inspired intriguing partnerships in the business community, even among those with competing interests. When the women's ministry needed transportation for every day needs, three local car dealerships—Jim Elkins, owner of Elkins Chrysler-Mitsubishi; Tony Fisher, owner of University Ford; and Gene Smith, manager of Hendrick's Chevrolet, teamed up to buy, what else—a Dodge van for the Mission.

In 2004, when the Mission's main cooking stove caught fire, local television stations ran the story, with Ernie explaining that the replacement cost of the commercial stove would be $4,000.

By the next day, six companies and individuals had offered to purchase the new stove. Gail called one man who sent a check for the stove to tell him someone else had already

Competitors work together to provide transportation for homeless women and children. (L–R) Gene Smith with Hendricks Chevrolet; Jim Elkins, owner of elkins Chrysler-Mitsubishi; the Mills; and Tony Fisher, owner of University Ford.

Roland Wilkins is a faithful volunteer who is always telling friends about the rescue mission.

purchased it. She thanked him for his kindness, and said she would be returning the check because he had designated it for that cause, and it had already been purchased.

"Don't you send it back," the man replied. "I trust your judgment that you all will find a good use for it."

Roland Wilkins, who has advised the Mission in it fundraising efforts, said one reason for that broad-based support is that it is easy to recognize that the preacher has a heart bigger than he is. He speaks to people in a down to earth way that reaches everyone, right down to the youngest of hearts.

He connects to children with his unique ability to make the message meaningful to them. Once, when collecting data, the Mission discovered that 50 percent of their female residents had eaten out of a trash can at one point.

"How many of you have helped your mommy take out the trash?" Ernie asked a group of kindergarten and grade schoolers. The exuberant youngsters all raised their hands.

"Have you ever had that bag break open before you got it outside? The trash gets on your clothes?" The children responded with a groan.

"And have you ever lifted up that lid of the trash can and had to hold your nose because of the smell?"

The groans grew louder and more dramatic.

"Have you ever been hungry and asked your mother for food and she told you to go to that trash can to find something to eat?"

Silence fell over the young crowd.

After that event was over, Ernie was walking out to his car, and he saw a boy sobbing next to his mother in the parking lot. The mom waved to Ernie to come over. She explained that the boy's father was an alcoholic, and he was touched by Ernie's testimony about his own father.

Ernie enjoys oppoturnities to tell others about the mission!

"He has a servant attitude and people recognize that sincerity. It just comes through in every presentation that he makes," Wilkins said.

Another thing that gives people confidence that their contributions will be used wisely is the remarkable fact that Ernie and Gail are still in charge after 30 years, still accomplishing the task they originally set out to do.

"It's quite unusual to have someone on board for 30 years who is the original founding member of a non-profit organization," Wilkins said, perhaps stating the obvious about a job that takes much more than a 9-5 commitment. They are no doubt the reason the Mission is often referred to as the heart of this diverse community.

Dichotomous might be a better word to describe Durham, at once a center for cutting edge technological, scientific, and medical research, just as in any urban center, there is another side of the story. A vast economic chasm divides it from the other end of the economic spectrum, where it is troubled by poverty, racial division and gang violence.

In recent years, according to U.S. Census figures, the city has jockeyed for position as the home to the most doctorate degrees per capita in the nation. Nicknamed the "City of Medicine," Durham boasts a physician-to-population ratio four times greater than the national average, according to the Durham Convention & Visitors Bureau.

It is not just that it is home to Duke University, and near two other research universities in Chapel Hill and Raleigh, that contributes to these statistics. It is also the city's close proximity to Research Triangle Park, touted as the world's largest research park. RTP, as it is known, encompasses 7,000 acres, with most of the more than 100 companies located there pursuing research and development in fields such as biotechnology, microelectronics, pharmaceuticals, telecommunications, public health and information technology. About half of the estimated 38,000 employees work for multinational corporations. With an estimated total payroll of $2.7 billion, the average salary for an RTP employee is listed as $56,000 on the park's website.

It is a far cry from the lives of many inner-city Durham residents.

Former Durham County Social Service Director Dan Hudgins compiled a detailed analysis of social problems at the other end of the economic spectrum that plague Durham. The city has the dubious distinction of having the highest school dropout rate in North Carolina. It also claims the highest urban crime rate and highest child poverty rate in North Carolina, according to those 2004 figures.

The Mission somehow bridges these otherwise disconnected segments of society and gives the diverse elements of the city something in common with its simple but powerful message of giving.

"This is far more than providing homeless people with food and shelter," said Wilkins, who spent nearly 30 years working in the development office of Duke University. "It does provide a difference beyond just training them for better jobs. It's a lifestyle. Ultimately, to the many of them who accept and believe Christ is their Savior, it offers eternal life, as well."

Precious children from our poor neightborhood received a backpack with school supplies during one of our "Back to School" parties.

In a neighborhood beleaguered by drugs, poverty, and crime, the Mission is a place where the haves and the have-nots can come together, and all have a good time. Four times a year, hundreds gather at the Mission for holiday and social events to celebrate Thanksgiving, Christmas, Easter, and back to school time. Along with the delicious meals, the dinners feature games for the inner city children, and an opportunity to share with them once again that God loves them. They are each intended to meet the needs of the working poor in Durham as well as the homeless.

Each August, just before school starts, hundreds of volunteers help run the Mission's annual Back to School Party for the community. In 2004, Golden Corral donated 2000 new JanSport backpacks, and the Mission bought hundreds more with donations. In all, the Mission gave out 2,300 new backpacks, filled with school supplies for children who cannot afford them.

Begun after the Columbine massacre in 1999, the Back to School party is one of the Mission's homeless prevention programs. Everyone can receive clothes, groceries, and a meal at the lively cookout, and of course the Gospel, which is presented at every event. Many have accepted Christ as their Lord and savior at these neighborhood gatherings—

Children delightfully receive and give out Easter baskets!

sometimes as many as 100 at a single event. Many families are able to head off missing a rent payment because of the little hand up the mission provides them.

At Easter, hundreds of underprivileged children receive Easter baskets and play games each year, while their parents can pick up groceries and clothing they need. Everyone is also invited for a free Christmas dinner of turkey and all the trimmings, and presents are given to the needy children in the community. Each event is preceded by a drive to collect what is needed—and the community has responded for 30 years with enough for everyone.

"Sometimes it comes down to that last minute donation, but God always provides," said Gail, remembering a volunteer who saw that several children had not received backpacks at one back to school event. She asked Gail to get the children's names, and the next day she delivered enough for those that didn't get one.

Then there was the Christmas when a man drove up and handed a baked turkey breast and a quart of gravy out of his car window to a waiting Mission worker. That dinner came down to just about the last slice of that turkey breast, despite the dozens

A little girl receives an educational toy at the annual Christmas dinner.

of whole turkeys that had been donated and prepared for that event.

The gatherings are known as much for the gifts they impart as for the community spirit they inspire.

Hundreds of volunteers help with the annual community dinners.

"I have found they have an outreach not only to the homeless and drug addicted, but also to the neighborhood of the marginally poor in northeast central Durham. It just shows what private enterprise can accomplish that government has not been able to do very well. When you can bring the neighborhood together, and give away 2,300 backpacks, and share their message and provide food and clothing, it's just remarkable," Wilkins said.

Thanksgiving is another much anticipated neighborhood bash, and a favorite time for fun and fellowship. Ironically, though, it is the event that attracts the most volunteers, but the fewest homeless people.

"A lot of families will let their loved ones come home for that holiday, even if they don't want them there the rest of the year," Gail said.

Even so, usually at least 1,000 meals are served, and it's worth it just to watch R. H. Ballard and a band of volunteers fry dozens of turkeys, grill hams, and cook mess-hall sized portions of vegetables in his unique assortment of giant pots.

Mr. R. H. Ballard (left)

Ballard can be found with his grills and 80-gallon cook pots at Mission events throughout the year. He is invariably there for Thanksgiving, Christmas—even though his wife of more than 53 years thought he might be done with those "working" holidays once he retired as IBM's Fire Marshall. He knows he is very fortunate to have such an understanding spouse.

"The Lord's done a lot for me. I try to do something for Him—help other people in dire need," said Ballard, who first volunteered to help prepare the Thanksgiving feast in 1994.

It is a familiar sentiment among mission volunteers who often say they get more than they give. Wilkins, who began volunteering for the Mission along with his wife in 1987, concurs.

"We have been blessed far more than what we've done for the organization."

*I*f it was a step of faith for Ernie and Gail to imagine outgrowing the Mission's modest quarters at the first Mission house, what happened in 2002 was a giant leap of faith.

Ernie had drawn up plans to expand the women's ministry by tearing down four houses the Mission owned in the neighborhood. He planned a new 15,000 square-foot building with 40 rooms. Once again, he learned, "Our vision wasn't big enough for what God had in mind."

Two miles away from the mission at 507 E. Knox Street, prominently overlooking the busy Interstate 85, stood the Durham Inn. It caught Ernie's attention because of a continuing legal battle waged by neighbors intent on having the haven for drug addicts and prostitutes obliterated from their neighborhood.

The Duke Park Neighborhood Association lobbied so effectively for their safety that a judge in February of 2002 actually proclaimed the public nuisance caused by the hotel more urgent than the owner's property rights. He ordered it demolished because of the constant barrage of shootings, rapes, robberies, and drug deals that were well documented by local police.

When Ernie took a closer look at the building, however, he saw something they couldn't possibly know. The rooms were identical in square footage and design to what Ernie had planned for the 40-room expansion, right down to the sinks located outside the bathroom area to make it convenient for more than one person getting ready in the mornings.

At 60,000 square feet, the motel was quadruple the size of his plans, and instead of 40 rooms, there were 130. He could triple the number of women served, have room for a new computer training lab and free up badly needed space at the downtown Mission.

Offices could be moved over to the inn, away from the beehive-like configuration on the second and third floors of the church building, where doors open into crowded cubicles and space is at a premium.

Despite the tacky blue exterior and the fact that it had become a haven for criminals, the concrete building was structurally sound. Ernie figured by renovating the inn, he could have four times the space at half the cost. It would also save the four Mission houses that wouldn't have to be torn down for a new building. The space it would open up at the Mission building and former women's shelter would allow the Mission to increase the number of men served by 50 percent.

The added room would also allow for the creation of a daycare center that would provide a nurturing and educational environment for the children at the Mission while their mothers train for their new careers. The possibilities seemed limitless.

The Old Durham Inn

"Something brought me here," Ernie said, arching an eyebrow heavenward.

But first he had to face a well-organized neighborhood group that was up in arms about the problems caused by drug addicts and prostitutes at the inn.

"Now, who do we serve? They are a major part of our clientele," Ernie said.

It's hard enough to convince a neighborhood to accept a shelter, but with the history of problems at the inn, he thought it would be a hard sell to get them to change their minds. Further compounding his worries was the fact that he was asking them to let the building remain standing in order to house homeless women—some of whom had been drug addicts and prostitutes.

"I went in fear and trembling," Ernie said.

He need not have worried. The Duke Park Neighborhood Association voted unanimously to support the Mission's plans.

Since then the larger community has embraced the project, soon re-named the "Good Samaritan Inn." Civic groups, businesses, and individuals immediately began adopting rooms, landscaping, and renovation projects to make it not just habitable, but homey.

"I truly believe God built this building for us 30 years ago," Ernie is fond of saying. He points to the room dimensions as well as the timing of availability of the building as reasons for his conviction on the matter. He repeats the clear conclusion he has come to about the Mission: "Our vision wasn't large enough."

Even people who may not share his strong faith say they are won over by his resolve to help the homeless turn barriers

The Durham Inn, once a dead end motel, becomes a place of new beginnings for homeless mothers and children.

Patrick Baker giving Ernie the occupancy permit for the Good Samaritan Inn.

into blessings.

"He's on a mission—literally," said Barry Ragin, who was vice president of the neighborhood association when Ernie made his appeal. "There was some talk about maybe getting a trail and some park land in there, but Ernie was three steps ahead of everyone. He has very strong convictions."

Patrick Baker, then Durham assistant city attorney, (now Durham city manager) who had argued the public nuisance case on behalf of the neighborhood, told Ernie he needed neighbor support before trying to get a judge to amend the hard-fought ruling.

"Ernie truly resurrected that building," Baker said.

Saving the building from the wrecking ball was only the first step, not the least of which was financing the venture.

Ernie asked the owner, Peak Properties, to finance the purchase. He agreed to finance $350,000 after a down payment of $400,000 was made within 90 days. It was summertime, normally a slow time for charitable donations. The post September 11th stock market was still falling in the summer of 2002. The prospect of a major fundraising success didn't look promising.

Still, Ernie contacted previous donors, sending letters outlining the opportunity, and the potential to triple the number of women the Mission could serve.

"We're having to turn away women and children regularly. Soon, we could have the luxury of something we've never had—an empty room," Ernie appealed to donors. He was certain three months was too short of a time frame for such an ambitious fundraising goal.

"I knew we'd be asking for an extension."

To Ernie's astonishment, in only 57 days, that $400,000 was in the bank drawing interest, with donors rallying around the project.

Chapter 25
JOINT COMMUNITY EFFORT REVIVES DEAD-END HOTEL

The transformation of the seedy hotel began immediately, with a dramatic outpouring of donations, volunteer labor, and materials to give it a new life.

- The outside of the old Durham Inn, notorious for its garish swimming-pool blue paint with a big rainbow across the side, was first on the list. Within three weeks of the purchase, the outside had a tasteful beige paint job, labor donated by John McKinney Paint Contractor of Durham. The Hillsborough Road Sherwin Williams store donated all of the paint.

- There was no central heating and cooling system in the kitchen, dining room, and lobby areas, which were carved out of the hotel lobby, coffee shop, and six former hotel rooms to meet the needs of the Mission. The Tri-County Heating and Air Conditioning Contractors Association stepped in, donating two new systems and installing them, along with new ductwork. "It's good for our hearts, and it's good for everybody," said Ron LaPann, the association's president. Ernie noted that it was an added blessing to see the association members, who are all competitors, working together for a community cause.

- The Durham Kiwanis Club and the Tobaccoland Kiwanis Clubs donated a pre-school playground and a school age play-  ground. Ronald McDonald House Charities of North Carolina gave $10,000 to finish the project. Lowe's Home Improvement donated chain link fence to enclose the playground.

- Rhonda Pollard, then the incoming president of the Durham Council of Garden Clubs, saw an opportunity to transform the motel property, dotted with scrub pine trees and weeds, into a beautifully landscaped garden area. The garden clubs purchased and planted six mature 25 and 30-foot-tall  shade trees. Always enthusiastic, she hardly expected her efforts would spur a groundswell of support from all over the community. By the time it was finished, in April, 2005, on behalf of the Durham Council of Garden Clubs, Pollard, accepted the North Carolina Garden Club's Award for an outstanding landscaping project. It's reputation grew, and in May, Anne Brown, The North Carolina Garden Club President accepted another award on behalf of the Durham Council from the South Atlantic Region of the National Garden Club, which is comprised of garden clubs in North Carolina, South Carolina, Virginia, West Virginia, and Kentucky. The garden was then recognized with the National Garden Club's Landscaping Award as the best landscaping project by any garden club in the country.

Pollard had started it all of, first seeking assistance from North Carolina State University's Assistant Professor Dr. Pat Lindsey, whose landscape design class adopted the project and drew up a master landscape plan for the two acres. They based their ideas directly on interviews they conducted with the homeless women at the Mission. They learned the women wanted peace and tranquility in their lives, with the sound of running water cascading over a waterfall. The result included a gazebo, a seven-foot fountain and a graceful sculptured metal bench in the shape of a butterfly.

• Cathy Lindsey, Pat's sister, owner of Lindsey Land-

scaping in Apex, called and enlisted the help of other nurseries and land-scapers to donate much of the plant material. Over a period of months, she organized and supervised the installation of dozens of donated shrubs and hundreds of ornamental plants, along with 10,000 square feet of Bermuda sod.

- Cathy Lindsey persuaded a lawn care company to provide a one-year contract to fertilize and spray the grass.

- The City of Raleigh donated many truckloads of mulch, also at Lindsey's request. She was able to get two landscaping and grading companies to donate their trucks and drivers to haul the mulch.

- Volunteers from the University of North Carolina, North Carolina Central University, N.C. State and Duke University—all fierce competitors on the court—pitched in to create a natural sanctuary for the homeless women and children at the inn.

- Mission board member Tom Williams, owner of T. L. Williams Grading Contracting in Raleigh, made it possible by eliminating flooding and erosion problems in

the garden. His company installed a critical drainage system. He also donated the installation of a walking trail that measures one-tenth of a mile so the women can keep track while they are walking for exercise.

- Kevin Sullivan, pastor of Family Baptist Church in Iron Mountain, Michigan, who used to work in the area as a brick mason before going into the ministry, brought 20 church members to work at the inn as an inner city mission project. Although rain prevented them from completing the beautiful work they began on several brick pillars at the entrance, Rev. Sullivan said: "My church members returned home from the trip with renewed spirit, as if they had been in a revival."

- Robby Oakley, owner of Oakley Masonry in nearby Garner, volunteered to finish building the brick pillars. The Mission installed wrought iron fencing and gates to connect the stately pillars and create an inviting entrance.

- Both Durham Home Depot stores donated materials for wooden arbors to define the sanctuary, with employees jumping at the chance to volunteer in their time off to do the arbor installation.

- The North Pointe Home Depot donated materials, and employees donated labor to renovate a room to be a beauty shop for the women.

- Not to be outdone, the Home Depot on Mount Moriah Road in Durham gave the Mission an in-store credit of $18,000 to purchase materials for renovating the inn.

- Paul Van Raay, an engineer at the Research Triangle Park-based East Coast Division of Cisco Systems told his co-workers that the Good Samaritan Inn needed a phone system. The employees raised enough money to buy the company's newest computerized IP phone system with their substantial employee discount, and donated the extensive labor to re-wire the entire building. Seeing the enthusiasm from its employees, the corporation took note, donating additional computer equipment to the project. If the Mission purchased the system at retail, it would have cost more than $80,000.

- GlaxoSmithKline sent 125 employees to the Inn on a team building and community awareness project. Bill Shore, director of U.S. community partnerships for the company, is a Durham native, and spearheaded the $250,000 scholarship endowment for the Mission. He said the company fosters a culture of community involvement among its employees. The employees spent two and a half days on the company's clock painting 18 rooms and setting up furniture. GlaxoSmithKline paid to have the carpets steam cleaned, and purchased shower curtains, area rugs, towels, sheets, and blankets for each room. The company also supplied them with the company's toiletry items, such as Aquafresh Toothpaste, and other personal hygiene products. GlaxoSmithKline then donated top of the line furniture from a company guest house it sold, including sofas, bedroom sets, and a mahogany dining room suite that now furnishes the Inn's conference room.

- Verizon Vice President of External Affairs, Joe Foster, was instrumental in obtaining a company grant of $3,000 for the Mission to help purchase some of the new Dell computers for the state-of-the-art computer lab on the third floor of the inn. Verizon also bought four laptops, an overhead video projector and screen for the lab.

- The Legacy Group, a leadership training program in Cary, adopted the lobby and dining room. They painted walls and installed new track lighting. The group also pur-  chased ceramic tile flooring and paid a professional artist to create a lush garden mural on a wall in the dining room. The previously dark, cave-like entrance now is a bright, cheery, and sooth- ing welcome area.

Larry Jacobs to the rescue.

The heartwarming support of these and many other companies was multiplied by the time donated by employees of the corporations and individuals from the community.

Many other groups, from Boy Scouts to Sunday school classes to individual families, adopted rooms at the inn to refurbish and furnish for the incoming homeless women and children.

In one instance, just as the work on the inside began, volunteers working to refurbish the hotel lobby into a din- ing room exposed a leak from a carport overhang which had rotted the wooden wall studs in one area along the wall facing Interstate 85.

"My heart just sunk," Ernie recalled.

Never one to dwell on disaster, Ernie quickly called Ja- cobs Glass Company in Durham to see how much it would cost to replace the entire 25-foot wall with windows, be- cause he wanted to make the enclosed room brighter.

"It won't cost you anything because my company will take care of that," replied owner Larry Jacobs. Jacobs also replaced several broken windows, and provided glass for interior renovations.

People seemed to think of everything.

One offer that was politely declined was from volun- teer Rodger Groff who wanted to buy Ernie a new suite of office furniture. "No thank you," Ernie said. One of the Mission residents, Cliff Mather, had built the large desk in

Rodger & Brownie Groff

his current cramped office out of a heavy oak door. He worked at a cabinet shop, and built it there, placing an understated wooden cross at the front. No other desk would ever be as special to him, Ernie said. He did accept new book cases and a comfortable office chair, though.

That so many people would donate their money and time to carefully decorate rooms and supply their needs—from the tasteful window treatments right down to the tooth brushes and teddy bears that wait in welcome for the women and their children—is amazing to the women who will live at the Good Samaritan Inn.

"It puts me in awe," said Donna Carrington, who was staying at the Mission with her three children. "You don't realize how many people are trying to do good for others."

Tears come to Gail's eyes as she turns to lock a door that is waiting for a new resident of the Inn. Taking one last peek at the lovely matching floral curtains and comforters that a volunteer painstakingly selected, she asks: "Can you imagine a mother, with her children, who have nothing and nowhere to go, coming into this room?"

It took Ernie and Gail Mills to imagine such a thing—and to turn it into a living testimony of faith and obedience.

*I*n Luke 4:18, Jesus said, "*The Spirit of the Lord is upon me, because he hath anointed me to preach the gospel to the poor; he hath sent me to heal the brokenhearted, . . . *"

It is not surprising that Luke 4:18 is Ernie's favorite Bible verse. After nearly four decades of preaching to the poor, it is clearly the defining verse of his life's work. He has provided a place where those without hope can grasp hold of their salvation.

To those who knew him back in Frog Level as a youth, before he became a Christian, the idea of Ernie Mills becoming a preacher was an unexpected turn of events, to say the least.

Schoolmates generally pause in search of a diplomatic answer when asked if they were surprised when they first heard he had gone into the ministry.

"I don't know what I would have predicted for him, but it wouldn't have been that," smiled high school chum Lynwood Stocks.

Classmates from his Winterville High School 40th class reunion in 2004 said Ernie was a bit of a class cutup. Never a trouble maker, Ernie was a fun-loving prankster, with a wry sense of humor. He was equally as serious

40-year class reunion at Winterville.

with his studies, too. That's why, after high school, when they all heard he was headed to Bob Jones University instead of Pitt Community College, a lot of them scratched their heads.

"He was always such a nice person, but I don't know if I would have expected that," said Becky Maye, who also attended the same school. "But when the Lord gets a hold of you, you never know what may happen."

Indeed, perhaps no one was more surprised than Ernie was at the transformation that took place the summer between high school and college. He became a Christian quite unexpectedly, and followed his heart into the ministry. But, he said, he is only part of the story.

"It was nothing that I planned. It was God's will and His providence that we're here. If anything had developed in Durham, it definitely would have been nothing like it is today without Gail. She complements me in so many areas where I am weak. Not many husband and wife teams can actually work together. This Mission is as much her as it is me. She's my faithful sidekick," he said. "She is really the heart of the Mission. I do a lot of dreaming. She does a lot of work."

Thousands are grateful that the inseparable pair stuck by their convictions and stayed faithful to a mission that has helped so many for more than 30 years and counting.

On November 18, 2004, at a surprise 60th birthday party for Ernie at the Durham Rescue Mission, several people who have been helped expressed their gratitude.

"I've come a very, very long way," said Mission resident Candace Bailey. "In my heart, I had a real emptiness that I built a wall around. It took me coming to the Durham Rescue Mission to break down that wall. I cannot thank you enough for that. The Durham Rescue Mission has given me the opportunity to be free. I am so grateful that the Durham Rescue Mission was here when it was my season to surrender my addiction."

Brenda VanHook had only been at the mission a few months when she stood before the congregation to wish Ernie a happy 60th birthday.

"I asked my probation officer to put me in jail because I was sick of running. She called the Durham Rescue Mission, and a bed opened up 10 minutes later. Before I got here, I doubted God because I had turned my back on Him," VanHook said.

William Brewer said that when he arrived at the Durham Rescue Mission, he was clinically depressed.

"I was in detox for alcoholism. I was suicidal, and I was going to end it. I had lost my wife, my kids, my material possessions. My brother's got no respect for me," and on and on the list of troubles went, he said.

"I came here looking for some peace. You're really helping a lot of people," Brewer said.

Mission resident Earl said he had run out of places to turn.

"The VA closed the door in my face. Here, I learned God can still open doors that man cannot," he said. "I've been strung out on everything – women, drugs, alcohol. I didn't have parents since I was 8. But here I realized the void I was trying to fill was from missing Christ, Jesus."

It wasn't just people who were once homeless who have benefited from Ernie and Gail's Christian example.

Though Ernie's nephew Richard Carr, Jr. had been coming to the Mission since he was a small boy with his father, Richard, and mother Ellen, (Ernie's sister) he really didn't understand what it was about.

Then, while studying landscape management at N.C.

State University in Raleigh, Rich stayed with Ernie and Gail in their home.

"I was a typical Christian teenager. I had one foot in the world and one foot in church. Then I stayed with them, and I saw a Christian life being lived before me. Their love is so sacrificial; you can't help but see it."

During his stay, Rich participated in the family devotions around the breakfast table, along with Ernie Junior and Bethany, as they studied the book of Proverbs. Ernie and Gail noticed how the study seemed to get a hold of Rich and led him to get serious about living the Christian life.

In 2004, Rich and his wife, Jennifer, moved to Durham, and Rich serves as landscape manager for the Mission. He is also bi-lingual and does much of the Mission's Hispanic outreach.

In a poem written by in honor of Ernie's 60th birthday, one resident put it this way: "My life is forever changed by the grace you've shown God had for me."

"We found security here. Some of us felt suicidal," said Helen Dixon. "Preacher Mills, thank you for answering the call."

With tears threatening, Ernie quoted scripture in response to the moving expressions of love they showed.

"My mind goes back over there to Third John, chapter 1, verse 4: 'I have no greater joy than this to hear of my children walking in the light.' To look out on the sea of this body of people and to see the work that you have let God do in your lives—you are a blessing," Ernie said.

None of it would be possible without the Lord, he said.

Ernie never misses an opportunity to credit God with how the Mission has grown.

With that unswerving adherence to the Bible, by 2004, it's 30th year of operation, the Mission grew into an extensive

Arial shot of Rescued Treasures Thrift Shoppe

campus of more than 34 houses and 10 vacant lots used for gardens, with the church building the hub of many daily activities intended to train residents how to live productive lives. Just two miles away stands the 130-room Good Samaritan Inn, and only three miles in the opposite direction, the Mission is set to open a 10,000-square-foot "Rescued Treasures Thrift Shop" in 2005. In 1974, the mission could house 12 men. Thirty years later, in 2004, the Mission averaged 160 men, women, and children per night. The Good Samaritan Inn will triple the number of women and children the Mission can help.

Looking back on his beginnings, the son of a share-cropper, bootlegger, and alcoholic father, no one is more surprised about what God has used his life to achieve than Ernie Mills.

"I never really dreamed the Mission would advance beyond the first two-story house we bought," Ernie said. "I was content with that."

The message on the lobby wall of the Good Samaritan Inn best tells the story of how the Durham Rescue Mission was possible. In bold letters, Psalms 118:23 reads:

*"This is the Lord's doing,
it is marvelous in our eyes."*

Appendix

A CHRONOLOGY OF THE DURHAM RESCUE MISSION

1973 – Ernie and Gail Mills move to Durham in hopes of starting a rescue mission

1974 – Opened shelter for men at 1301 E Main St.

1978 – Moved to 1201 E Main St. to expand

1993 – Opened shelter for mothers with preschool children

1997 – Opened shelter for families

1998 – Opened shelter for single women

2002 – Purchased & renovating Good Samaritan Inn for women and children

2002 – Purchased 10,000-square foot building for future thrift store

2005 – Opened Good Samaritan Inn at 507 E Knox St.

2006 – Opened Rescued Treasures Thrift Shoppe at corner of Hwy 55 & Cornwallis Rd.

2006 – Mission received a $500,000 grant from SunTrust through Federal Home Loan Bank of Atlanta to renovate west wing of Good Samaritan Inn

Index